SPORTS MEMORABILIA:

A Guide to America's Fastest Growing Hobby

by

John A. Douglas

Over 375 sports collectables illustrated in full color. Hundreds more are shown and described in black and white. Also included are a glossary of terms, and an easy-to-use index.

An accompaning price guide to this book is available at fine bookstores everywhere.

Dedication

To my Dad and Barney . . . for having the patience to take a young boy to sports events I still remember today; and to my Mother, who for many years resisted the urge to throw away the memories.

Library of Congress Catalog Card Number
76-24040
ISBN: 0-87069-202X

Published by
WALLACE-HOMESTEAD BOOK CO.
Box BI
Des Moines, Iowa 50304

Most items pictured in this book are from the author's collection. They are not for sale. Persons who have items they wish to sell, or questions they would like answered, may contact the author by writing to The Wallace-Homestead Book Company. Please enclose a stamped, self-addressed envelope.

Table of Contents

Acknowledgements

I am very appreciative of the cooperation that was given by the following teams, companies and individuals. Without their efforts, this book would not be possible.

The Philadelphia 76'ers
The Buffalo Bills
The Kentucky Colonels
The St. Louis Blues
The Houston Rockets
The Miami Dolphins
The Kansas City Kings
The San Diego Chargers
The Chicago White Sox
The Green Bay Packers
The New Orleans Saints
The Chicago Bears
The Los Angeles Dodgers
The Cleveland Cavaliers
The Atlanta Braves
The Milwaukee Brewers
The San Diego Padres
The San Francisco Giants
The New York Rangers
The Pittsburgh Penguins
The Kansas City Royals
The New York Yankees
The Philadelphia Phillies
The Toronto Toros
The Philadelphia Eagles
The Spirits of St. Louis
The Minnesota Twins
The California Angels
The Atlanta Hawks
The Detroit Lions
The Montreal Canadiens
The Minnesota Fighting Saints
The Detroit Tigers
The Kansas City Scouts
The Philadelphia Flyers
The Cleveland Crusaders
The Montreal Expos
The Houston Oilers
The Denver Broncos

The Pittsburgh Steelers
The Pittsburgh Pirates

The Wilson Sporting Goods Co.-Mr. Ray Kolas
The Spalding Company-Miss Mia Dodge
KTMJ Television-Miss Sharon Naughton
The Pinkerton Tobacco Company-Mr. K.D. Wanamaker
The Topps Chewing Gum Co.-Mr. Berger

Frank Schlueter
Jack Urban
Gene Leggitt
Fred Schwengel
Dave Bradley
Clyde Oxenreider
Orlando Itin
Mickey Mantle
Mike Stenzel
Ed Budnick
Lee Gobble
John Sullivan
Pat Quinn
Steve Hepfer
Dick Millerd
Dick Dobbins

Special Thanks To:

Type-O-Graphics Two, Inc.

Norm Cohen
Bob Mathias
Dan Even
Jann Williams-Wallace-Homestead
Bob Lyon-Wallace-Homestead
Richard Egan
Jack Thompson
Cover Art-Ken Prestley

Foreword

"We have some salt of our youth in us"

- William Shakespeare

Remembering, say some psychologists, is not healthy. How wrong they are. For in recalling the past, we put the present in perspective.

Nostalgia is in vogue. How fitting in this, the 200th anniversary of our Nation, that we have a book devoted to the recapturing of times and things nearly forgotten. For that is what collecting is.

Many persons - myself included - are not collectors in the card-carrying sense, but still cherish the things of long gone times.

I have saved many momentos of my earlier days, and often look at those photos, clippings, and awards to recall the feats and friendships of those times. They make recollection more vivid and enjoyable.

Today, nearly three decades after my first Olympic trip, I still receive requests for autographs and information. I've always felt obligated to answer these. I'm flattered that people still remember; and proud that I was able to represent the country I so love.

These memories - plus the momentos of those past days - are my collection.

Bob Mathias

Washington, D.C.
March 9, 1976

In 1948, at the age of 17, Bob Mathias won the gold medal in the Decathlon at the London Olympics. Four years later, he became the only man to win that Olympic event twice.

Mr. Mathias has starred in four major motion pictures and a T.V. series. In 1966, he was elected to his first of four terms as a member of the U.S. Congress. He served on the Agriculture and Foreign Affairs committees.

Among the many awards he has received are the AAU's Sullivan Award, the U.S. Junior Chamber of Commerce award as one of America's ten most outstanding young men, and election to the National Track and Field Hall of Fame in 1974.

Introduction

Many veteran collectors of sports memorabilia have had a difficult time believing the transition that has taken place within this hobby in the last 5-10 years. What was once a very subdued, gentlemanly pastime of trading bubble gum cards with others through the mails is now the current nostalgic rage across the country. The countless magazine and newspaper articles that have been written about collectors and sports collecting, television coverage, conventions being held almost every weekend in some part of the country, expansive publications devoted to the interests of sports collectors; all are examples of this fast-growing hobby.

No longer is the trading card the only item that interests collectors. Articles such as programs, yearbooks, autographs, postcards, and even uniforms have become specialty areas for countless new recruits to the hobby.

On the following pages a general overview of this hobby, the collector and what is being collected is presented. Whenever possible,

illustrations are used for easy recognition by the reader. No attempt has been made to include every item that exists, or is being collected. Not only would this be an impossible task, but if it were possible, this book would be outdated by now. New items are being found by collectors each week.

Some revolutionary approaches have been taken in several chapters in organizing the material presented. It is hoped that this more logical approach to classification and organization will allow a greater number of people to better understand the descriptives used.

It is further intended that this information will provide a basis for an even greater involvement and enjoyment in what has become America's fastest-growing hobby. The 15,000 serious collectors currently participating in this hobby provide the tangible proof that this pastime has indeed arrived!

John A. Douglas
March 7, 1976

The Author

John Douglas bought his first package of bubble gum cards as an eight year-old in 1956. Together with other kids on the east side of Detroit, he spent many a summer afternoon buying, trading and flipping cards. While living in Detroit he attended hundreds of professional games that proved to strengthen his appreciation of sports.

He was graduated from Eastern Michigan University in January, 1971, with a B.S. degree in Journalism. He earned an M.A. degree in August, 1972. Douglas received numerous University honors for his activities on campus and in the community. His collection of sports memorabilia is one of the largest, and most diversified in the Hobby. Areas within his collection of special emphasis are autographs and uniforms. It is hoped someday that his equipment and display items will form the basis for a non-profit sports museum.

Douglas authors the "Yesterday's Hero" column in **The Baseball Bulletin,** and "JAD's Jury" in the **Sports Collectors News.** He has served the Great Plains Sports Collectors Association as its first president. He has designed several sets of trading cards for Sheraton Hotels and for 'CoolPapa' Bell, to name a few.

Sports Tickets

Since the inception of professional sports some 100 years ago, an admission price has been charged to the public to see the contest. In almost all instances, the proof of admission was a ticket. The vast majority of all these admission tickets that were issued for thousands of different sporting events were never saved by the owner. Those who did tend to save their stubs were the type of people that never threw anything away. The income tax law — the 16th Amendment — was ratified in 1913. The public began to save receipts from their expenditures, and that included stubs from the sporting events they attended.

While sports ticket collecting is still an area that has relatively few followers, it is catching the interest of an increasing number in the hobby; especially younger, beginning collectors. The ticket stub is, as a general rule, inexpensive, easy to acquire, and to store or display.

The two basic categories in this area of the hobby are full tickets and ticket stubs. Full tickets are those that were not used for admission by the purchaser. Tickets in their full form are a scarcity. Most people that purchase tickets use them — especially for the important games. The ticket stub is the portion of your ticket that the taker gives to you as proof of admission; and often so that you can find your seat.

Ticket values coincide with those of programs as they are based on the importance of the event (a World Series is more valuable than a regular season game), attendance (supply and demand), age, condition. The variable that is unique to the ticket is whether it is full, or a stub.

A recent trend in ticket printing — the computer — may provide the boom, or demise, of this division of collecting. Most collectors view the computer-printed ticket as a 'black sheep'. Some are predicting that someday all tickets will be printed by computer type. This will either diminish interest in ticket collecting because of this standardization; or cause a mad rush for the older tickets that are now in circulation. Only time will answer this dilemma.

There are presently more collectors interested in baseball tickets than any other sport. Some of the other specialties that have support, though, include boxing tickets (often very large, with distinct shapes and designs), Rose Bowl tickets, Indy 500 tickets (the most colorful), NFL-AFL Super Bowl tickets, and certain college football teams in specific sections of the country.

Tickets from franchises that are now defunct also are popular items. The recent collapse of the World Football League and the ABA plus the sudden and frequent actions involving teams in the WHA have further added interest.

In addition to the common ticket, some collectors prize their accumulations of press passes, or badges. These forms of identification, usually in the form of a pin, are issued for important events such as the Indy 500, the World Series, the Rose Bowl and baseball's All-Star game. They are made in very limited numbers, and are extremely difficult to acquire. Most members of the press are not willing to part with 'their' souvenir of the event.

On some occasions the performance of a single player can transform the value of a ticket from a few cents to dollars. For example, a stub from a basketball game held in Hershey, Pennsylvania in 1962 would not be an item of notoriety if it were not for the fact that Wilt Chamberlain scored 100 points in that game for the Philadelphia Warriors. Accomplishments such as this, increase the demand tremendously. Examples of other qualifiers to this category would be no-hitters, record-setting home runs, milestone hits, points, baskets, world records, etc.

One other unusual category in ticket collecting is comprised of tickets from games that were cancelled, or in some cases, never took place. Because of close pennant races, it is often necessary to print playoff tickets for more than one team in a division. The tickets are sold, and then refunds are made if the team fails to make the playoff series. Depending on sales, returns, non-returns and what the club decides to do with the tickets following audit, a value is determined. As was the case with the 1974 College All-Star football game, the game was cancelled.

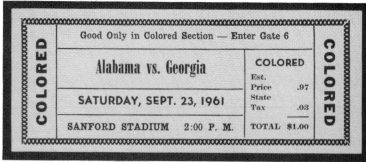

Collectors who own tickets such as this one are reminded that the South held on to many of its traditions until the mid-60's. Few collectables can surpass this one as a conversation piece.

This is a sample of a club ticket form that is put through a computer to add any variable information, such as section numbers, seat numbers, date, etc.

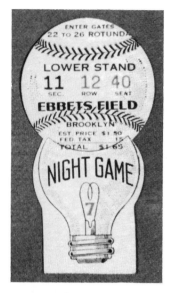

Night games were still an oddity in the early 50's; so the Dodgers employed this ticket design to remind fans of the starting time.

The rival Federal League lasted only two years. Ticket stubs, as well as any memorabilia from this operation, are very scarce.

Baseball fans still marvel at the architecture of Boston's Fenway Park. It opened in 1912. You could sit in the bleachers for two bits.

The 1961 White Sox tickets contained the pictures of different players on the back sides. Fans would often go to the booth requesting a seat in the "J. C. Martin Section," or the "Early Wynn Section." Three or four players were featured each home stand. These are popular even with card collectors.

The Dodgers moved into Dodger Stadium in 1962 and utilized this unusual admission pass to commemorate their new home.

8

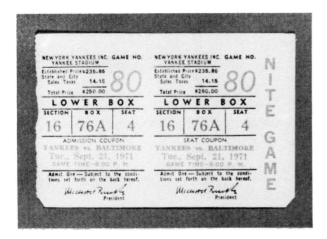

Baseball season ticket holders often receive their tickets in a coupon book form. This is a full 'ticket' for this particular game.

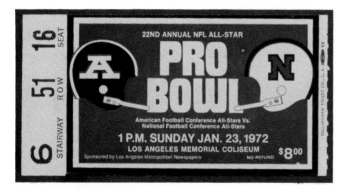

A stub from the annual Pro Bowl game matching stars from football's two conferences.

This unique full ticket was used for the first game in the Angels new stadium in Anaheim.

The crowd set new attendance records for college basketball. The undefeated Bruins with Lew Alcindor came to the Astrodome in 1968 only to be upset by Elvin Hayes' memorable performance.

Metal press badges are issued each year for the Indy 500. Each pin has a unique design, the year of the race, and an individual serial number for each press member. The third pin was the only such pin issued at the Pocono 500 in 1971.

The Super Bowl ticket is usually large, colorful, and in demand by collectors.

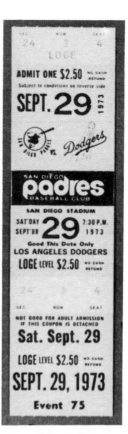

A number of collectors ordered this particular ticket through the mail because it was supposed to be the Padres last game in San Diego. Their rumored move to Washington, D. C. never materialized.

This full ticket is from the fourth game of the 1974 WHA championship. The owner decided not to attend the deciding game, and the Aeros' subsequent celebration.

The World Football League is now history. Full tickets such as this one are as plentiful as stubs.

Fans who attended this game in 1965 saw baseball history as Sandy Koufax threw a perfect game.

The most popular, and highest priced, tickets are those from World Series games. This sampling includes stubs from the 1929 and '31 Series (notice similarity in design), the 1958 Braves-Yanks tilt, a full ticket from the 1959 classic; Denny McLain's only win for the Miracle Tigers of 1968, and a full ticket from Pittsburgh's 'no show' of 1970.

The Reds utilized press tags for the 1970 All-Star game.

The Chicago Cardinals are now in St. Louis, but many Chicagoans still remember Charley Trippi and Lamar McHan.

The College All-Star football game is now an American tradition. Most of pro football's greats have played in this game, on one side and/or the other. Shown is a ticket from the 1964 game, and one from the cancelled 1974 event. The 1974 ticket was for the seat to be occupied by a former All-Star performer, and then Vice President of the United States, Gerald Ford.

Older football tickets, such as this one, from major status schools are popular with collectors. This ticket would be more valuable in the Columbus or Champaign area.

The Chicago Bulls played their first game in the Windy City in 1966.

The St. Louis Browns are but a memory. This ticket is from their 'swan song' season-1953.

Few stadiums are as famous as Soldier Field in Chicago. This stub from the opening game in 1926 is enhanced by the fact that the game pitted Army against Navy.

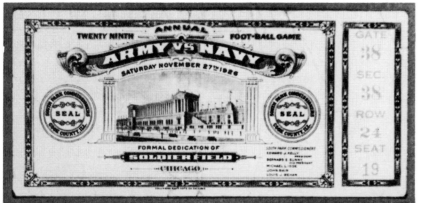

This unusual press box pass was issued by Northwestern in 1917.

This stub is from opening day 1974, at Cincinnati's Riverfront Stadium. The significance runs deeper than that, as Henry Aaron hit home run #714 to tie the Babe's record. A stub from the game he hit #715 would be worth twice the value of this one.

This lapel pin was issued to the press in 1968 by the Detroit Tigers for the World Series. It is unique in that the date of the series is not included as on other pins.

The tickets issued for the Indianapolis 500 are the most colorful of all sports tickets. The ticket includes a full-color picture of the previous year's winner and his car. Most Indy fans hang onto these.

Regularly scheduled baseball playoff series have been held since 1969. Although there is little difficulty in completing a set at this time; these may be as popular as World Series tickets in the future. This stub is from the '74 Dodger-Pirate series.

13

Equipment

The most unique area of sports collecting involves authenic equipment. The most prominent items classified in this category are professional uniform tops, or jerseys; baseball hats, bats and gloves; hockey sticks; and, football helmets. Other subsidiary items include minor league baseball equipment, college jerseys, and equipment from sports other than baseball, football, basketball and hockey.

For years young boys have smilingly returned from ballparks with broken bats from the afternoon's contest. Hockey sticks, often in two pieces, made many trips home from arenas in the hands of some happy fan. A professional player would occasionally give a jersey to a neighbor. Now, years later, all of these items are surfacing; and finding their way into the hands of collectors.

While there have been hundreds of thousands of Hank Aaron cards printed during his long career, there have only been approximately 100 uniforms made for his use. Although a player goes through many bats, the total number comes no where near the number of trading cards printed of him. This unique characteristic has been an impetus for many collectors who pursue these items.

This, the newest area in sports collecting is also the most confusing. Prior to 1972, there were only a handful of collectors involved in this very specialized area of interest. Today, there is an ever-increasing number of hobbyists who are becoming involved. The number, though, is still relatively small in comparison to most other areas of collecting. Great difficulty in acquiring items, problems with storage, high prices, and dubious authenticity of many items have all contributed to this situation.

Unlike most other collectables, there are few hard and pat statements that can be made concerning the identification of authenic items. It would be of immeasurable help if statements such as these could be made, "All major league bats are made by the X Company." "All professional football teams use Y Company helmets." "A legitimate major league baseball uniform must have the player's name sewn in the collar." Unfortunately, definitives such as these have no basis.

The two fundamental terms in equipment collecting are 'authenic' and 'sample.' Authenic sports equipment items are those that were once the property of the team, and were worn or used by the player in question. Authenic items carry a much higher value than those that are not. Sample items are identical reproductions of the same material that is used by the player or team. In recent years, hundreds of sample items have deluged the market. Ordered by collectors from the manufacturer, these are then sold or traded to unsuspecting collectors by unscrupulous individuals as 'authenic.' Only the very knowledgeable collector can differentiate between the authenic and reconstruction models.

The demise of the World Football League, and the death of several American Basketball Association and World Hockey Association franchises has poured hundreds of new items into the Hobby since 1974. Most of these were either sold by local sporting goods stores that had originally supplied the team, or by the Internal Revenue Service in payment for back taxes. The value of these items, though, has been diminished by the large supply available. Prices, in general, have declined on most equipment items since 1974. Items used by the better players, though, have increased slightly.

Major manufacturers of professional equipment include Wilson, Rawlings, Spalding, McAuliffe, Medalist-Sand Knit, McGregor, Hillerich & Bradsby, and Adirondack. Wilson Sporting Goods has been producing major league uniforms since the early 1930's, and still have most of the contracts with the baseball clubs. Medalist-Sand Knit and McAuliffe have come in to prominence since the double knit baseball uniforms were adopted in 1970. Hillerich & Bradsby's "Louisville Slugger" bats have dominated the majors for almost fifty years.

Values on sports equipment is dictated by authenticity, the status of the player who used it, age, style and condition. Baseball uniforms usually bring a higher price than other sports. All-Star and superstar players' items are much more valuable than those of a bench-sitter. Age is usually a factor, as older items are often difficult to locate. Flannel uniforms are more valuable than the new knits. Style changes can often dictate value. If a team used the same style uniform for ten years, then adopted a new style for two before buying a third version that was used for six; the 'two year' uniforms would exist in fewer numbers, and be more valuable. Items from defunct teams, with the exception of most WFL teams, have a higher price.

On the following pages a sampling of the items that are becoming common fixtures in the basements and rec rooms of collectors are shown. A few of the more common labellings are also pictured to assist the reader in establishing the authenticity of other similar items.

Shirts worn by All-Star caliber players are more valuable. Shown here, clockwise from upper left, are tops used by Boog Powell, Jim Bunning, Carl Yastrzemski and Harmon Killebrew. The pants that go with these shirts have little appeal to collectors. With a few exceptions, they have no unusual characteristics that distinguish pants from one team with those of another.

Items from franchises that have moved, or changed names a number of years ago are particularly difficult to obtain. Shown here are uniform tops from the Brooklyn Dodgers, Houston Colt .45's and the Milwaukee Braves.

Some collectors have a special interest in certain teams. Shown here are Detroit Tiger uniforms that span a fifteen year period. Clockwise, from upper left, home 1966; road 1958; road 1966; road knit 1972.

The older football jerseys, such as the J.C. Caroline Chicago Bear shirt on the right, did not carry the player's name on the back. The shirt on the left, worn by Bob DeMarco of the Miami Dolphins, is typical of the new mesh jerseys used by most teams today.

Year tags are not included on the hat bands. Style changes can often help to narrow the date of a cap's use. The top sequence shows two different Houston Astro hats. The one on the left was adopted in 1971; the right was used from 1965-70.

    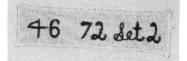

This is a sampling of major league baseball uniform labels. Clockwise, from upper far left; Wilson, 1958, size 44; Rawlings, set 1, 1965; Wilson, size 52, 1967, set 1; McGregor 1967, set 2; Wilson, size 46, 1972, set 2; Wilson, player name in shirt collar; Wilson, player name, year (70) and size in collar (44); McAuliffe 1965, size 44; Wilson, size 44, set 2, 1968.

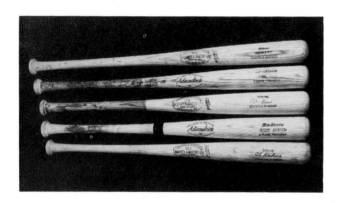

Major league bats owned by collectors are usually cracked. From the left, Al Kaline, Reggie Jackson, Pete Rose, Mike Schmidt, and Frank Howard. Note that some have the player's name printed, others include facsimile autographs. The Hillerich & Bradsby models all carry the line 'Powerized' just below the trademark. In addition, each players' bat has a special serial number stamped in the end of the knob.

College uniforms have little value, unless the player was an All-America. On left, a tear-away jersey worn by Pittsburgh's Tony Dorsett. On the right, Dick Van Arsdale's Indiana Top.

Collectors of basketball equipment form a very small group. Items such as this Nate Archibald Cincinnati Royals top, and Jerry Sloan's NBA All-Star Game jersey are considered valuable to these hobbyists.

16

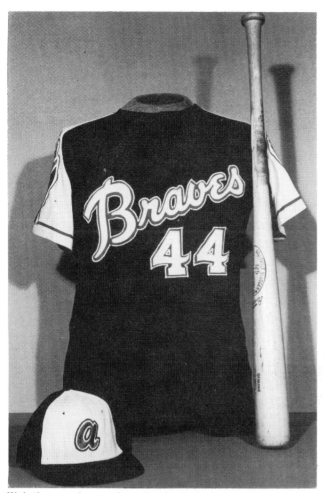

With the use of a manikin, a uniform almost 'comes to life,' and forms a very impressive display. This Henry Aaron uniform from 1972, along with bat and hat, is a good example. Most uniform collectors are also very involved in other display items.

Most baseball caps are made either by the KM Pro Company, or by New Era. Labels in the hat bands are shown for both models. KM also supplies reproductions to the public.

Uniforms from franchises that are now defunct have a higher market value. Clockwise, from top left; Seattle Pilots spring training and first part of season shirt, Washington Senators 1969, St. Louis Browns 1952 and Seattle Pilots 1969 regular season.

Pictured are three examples of shirts from short-lived franchises. The Michigan Stags were dead and gone before January 1, 1975; the Chicago Fire team in the WFL lasted one season; the life of the Chicago Cougars WHA team was not much longer.

Shirts worn by members of the Hall of Fame, of course, carry a higher value. This old top was used by Chicago Cub first baseman Frank Chance. The uniform was made by Spalding, and has his name sewn on the inside of the tail. (The Bear and Bat insignia is missing from the area inside the 'C.')

Professional football helmets form an impressive display with other equipment items. Fierce competition among manufacturers has led to these items now being guaranteed for a period of time. Teams no longer discard their broken and unrepairable headgear, but instead return them to the companies for replacement.

The ball used by the World Football League was a 'thing of beauty.' It was developed by the Spalding Company. The ball was a yellow-tan, with an orange stripe at both ends. Commissioner Gary Davidson's signature appeared on those used in 1974.

Periodicals and Annuals

The most common of all sports publications are the periodicals and annuals. Periodicals are issued weekly, monthly or quarterly and are distributed either by mail or at newsstands across the country. Almost every sports fan is familiar with such publications as **Sports Illustrated, The Sporting News** and **Sport.** Annuals are normally released just prior to the start of a sport's season. Popular examples include **Street & Smith's, Dell** and **True.** Most annuals, in certain aspects, can be considered guides. They often include team rosters, schedules and player biographies. They differ from those publications included in the Guidebook chapter of this book in that annuals also contain an editorial content that the others do not.

Periodicals and annuals, like many other publica-tion items, have not attained universal popularity with collectors. The major disadvantage to building a large collection of these magazines is the tremendous storage problem that results. Transacting trades with other collectors through the mails often results in a postage bill that exceeds the value of the publication itself.

The value of periodicals, as a general rule, is not substantial other than for the first few issues in a series. Value is dictated by supply and demand, age and condition. Prices for annuals are usually considerably higher than those of periodicals of comparable age and condition. While some collectors do not have adequate file space to save every issue of a periodical; they may have the room for a series of annuals.

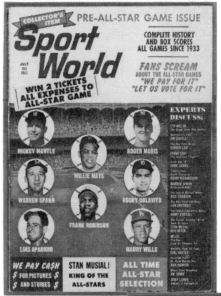

This is the first issue of SPORT WORLD, July, 1962. Sales were confined to newsstands.

One of the longest-running publications of any kind is THE SPORTING NEWS, which began printing in 1886. Commonly called "The Bible of Baseball," TSN has adopted a more universal sports coverage in recent years. Pre-1900 issues are very scarce, as are editions from the early part of this Century.

This initial issue of SPORTS STARS was on newsstands during the summer of 1962.

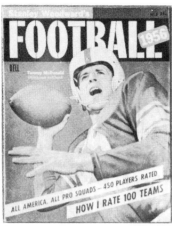

STANLEY WOODWARD'S FOOT-
BALL ANNUAL, published by Dell,
was issued from 1949 through the
early 60's when it became the DELL
FOOTBALL ANNUAL.

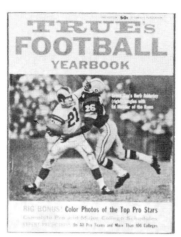

The TRUE FOOTBALL YEAR-
BOOK wa published from 1950-53.
After a two year absence, it has been
issued annually since 1956.

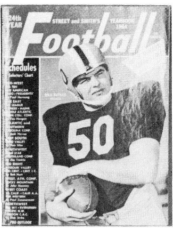

The most popular college football
annual is issued by STREET &
SMITH'S. The first volume appeared in 1940.

The DELL BASKETBALL ANNUAL
is one of many such magazines that
appear on newsstands in October.

Pictured is the cover from the first
STREET & SMITH'S BASKETBALL
YEARBOOK, published in 1957.

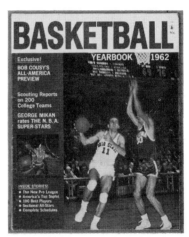

Popular Library Inc. issued basketball yearbooks in the late 50's and
early 60's. This 1962 issue features
a cover photo of Jerry Lucas.

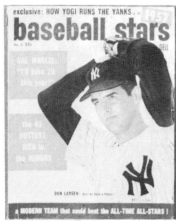

This edition of BASKETBALL STARS
is volume one of a number issued by
Dell.

This 1958 issue of SPORTS REVIEW
was the eighteenth issued, and the
fourth special baseball edition.

The STREET & SMITH'S BASE-
BALL YEARBOOK has been published each year since 1941.

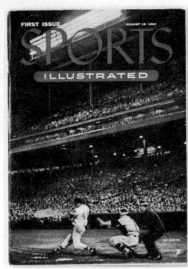 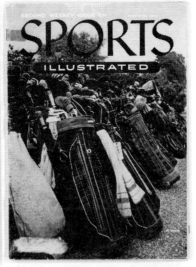

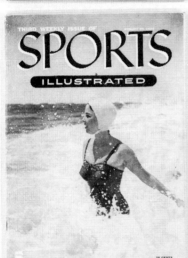 

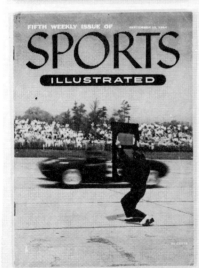 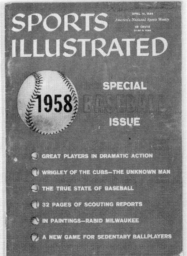

SPORTS ILLUSTRATED cover reproductions by permission of the publisher, TIME INC.

The most popular sports periodical of all time has been SPORTS ILLUSTRATED. The first issue, pictured in the upper left hand corner, was dated August 16, 1954. This first edition was mailed in a large envelope to subscribers of other Time-Life publications. It is very unusual to find one with a mailing label attached to the cover. This issue is popular with collectors for another reason; it contains a three page color foldout that pictures 27 1954 Topps baseball cards. An accompanying article outlines the legal battles that were taking place in 1954 between Topps and Bowman. Much harder to find are the early issues that followed the first. Pictured here are issues two, upper right; issue three, middle left; issue four middle right; and, issue five, bottom left. By this time the magazine had established a definite subscription list. Certain regular issues of SPORTS ILLUSTRATED are in greater demand. The annual baseball issue, bottom right; college and professional football issues; and the Sportsman of the Year issue are a few examples.

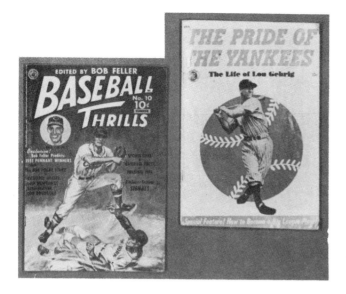

Baseball! personalities were featured in comic book form in the early 50's. On the left, a Bob Feller issue. The issue pictured on the right outlines the life of Lou Gehrig.

The first issue of SPORT appeared on newsstands in September, 1946. This issue, shown here on the left, featured a picture of Joe DiMaggio and his son on the cover. Other early issues, such as this April, 1948 edition with Ted Williams on the front, are also collected by hobbyists.

The SPORT ANNUAL, which is on the newsstands each December, highlights the top sporting events from the previous year. These editions provide a concise history of memorable accomplishments.

A very popular sports collectable are the old issues of BASEBALL MAGAZINE, published from 1908 to 1957. The Magazine appeared again in 1964 and '65, but has not been seen since. On the right, the July, 1956 issue. Pictured on the left is the November, 1936 edition.

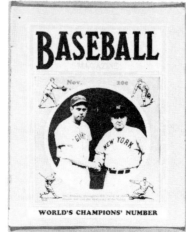

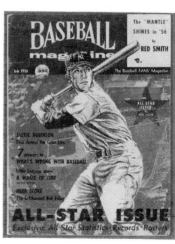

THE BASEBALL BULLETIN published its first edition in January of 1975. The monthly tabloid includes features and views on the sport of baseball.

The main components of SPORTS ILLUSTRATED has always been its excellent, full-color photography. Some covers seem to capture more than just a sporting event. This feature of Lombardi on the shoulders of Jerry Kramer needs no further explanation.

THE BASEBALL DIGEST has been published monthly since 1942. Older editions, such as this May, 1946 issue, are difficult to find and bring a good price to the seller. More recent issues, July 1960 edition shown, are inexpensive, and in ready supply.

Books

Books written on sports topics are very popular with some collectors. Instead of donating the read copies, collectors opt to save them for future reference or to read again at some later date. The pre-1900 books, though, are very much collectors items. Printed in limited quantities, and surviving hundreds of opportunities to have been discarded, these original works are now in great demand.

Books on baseball have the most interest, but old football printings finish a close second. Three of the most sought after baseball editions were written by Henry Chadwick in the 1866-1889 period. These volumes, in good condition, bring prices close to $50 each. An original copy of Ernest Thayer's "Casey at the Bat," published in 1901 is also very much in demand. Books written on the sport of football by such legendary persons as Edgar Allen Poe and Walter Camp are 'ultimates' with collectors of gridiron memorabilia.

The value of sports books is dictated by the length of the press run, condition, the status of the author, and whether or not the edition was autographed by the author.

Pictured here are some of the more photogenic recent sports editions. Older editions, very plain in cover appearance, are being overlooked only for artistic reasons.

Many recent books are actually worth less than their cover prices because of sales run by bookstores and publishers' clearing houses. That does not, however, diminish the enjoyment they have provided to readers.

The "Official History of the National League," published in 1951, and written by Charles Segar, is 96 pages in length. The book contains hundreds of photographs that highlight the first 75 years of the League. Included are 60 reprints of tobacco trading cards.

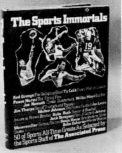

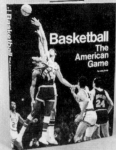

Pictorial histories of the various sports provide a great escape to readers. They are usually produced in smaller quantities than novels, or books that are eventually printed in paperback form.

Most trivia fans have purchased a copy of "The Sports Answer Book." Sports collectors, in general, are some of the most knowledgable persons on facts, figures and historical accounts of sporting events.

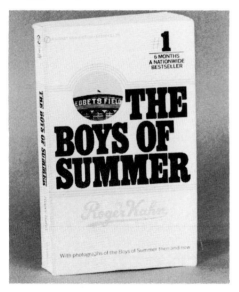

Paperback books have little monetary value. Most collectors, though, have read the nostalgic accounts of the Brooklyn Dodgers in "The Boys of Summer," and have kept their copies.

This pictorial summary of the 1972 Canada-Russia Hockey Series was printed in 1973.

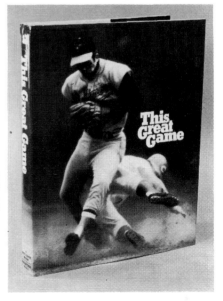

Books on baseball are the most popular with sports collectors. Whether those books focus on individuals, teams, ballparks or statistics, the sports collector is usually interested to the point of purchasing a copy.

Guidebooks

Guidebooks are yet another area of specialization for the sports collector. Fans interested in statistics, records and other pertinent data have accumulated these publications as a functional aid. In addition to the guides issued on a nation-wide basis, there are also media/press books printed by individual teams for the use of the press.

The most common, and popular, general baseball guides are those issued by the **Sporting News**. (1942-press). This type of all-inclusive guide was also issued in past years by the Reach Company (1883-1939), the Spalding Company (1877-1939), and the Barnes Company (1945 and '46) to name a few.

College and professional football guides are also very popular with collectors. The "Spalding College Football Guides" were issued from 1885 through 1940. Many of the early editions command premium prices. The NCAA has issued a guide annually since 1941. These are found today in good supply. The most common professional guidebooks are those issued by **The Sporting News** and the "NFL Manual" (1941-present), printed by the National Football League's office.

Professional, as well as most college teams, have issued press guides for many years. The press guide took on a more important meaning with the emergence of television as bona-fide medium in the early 50's. The Age of Television opened a new dimension for sport, and created new demands on the public relations offices of every club.

Media guides and programs in some cases are the only proof that certain teams ever existed. I know you all will remember the Minnesota Muskies entry in the ABA; or the Ottawa Civics WHA team that lived for a few weeks. How about the Memphis Sounds, the Philadelphia Blazers, or the Michigan Stags?

The values of sports guides are based on the age of the publication, condition, scarcity, and in the case of club-issued guides, the lifespan of the team itself. With the exception of the first few baseball **Sporting News Guides,** Dope Books, Record Books, etc., they would easily fit into the budget of most collectors. As a general rule, media guides issued by the teams are inexpensive; but, unless a collector limits his interests to one or two sports, the cost is prohibitive because of the large number of clubs in each category. The **Spalding** and **Reach** guides are considered scarce, and command a top price; as do most all other guides issued prior to 1940.

Media guides from championship teams are in higher demand and, therefore, demand a higher price. Some guides are relatively easy to obtain because the clubs have taken notice of the sports collector and are now offering their issues to the general public at a moderate price. Still others are combining media information into a yearbook format to reach a larger market with the average fan, while eliminating most costs associated with issuing a seperate publication for media people.

In determining value, condition is very important. With any publications, all pages should be intact, with both a front and back cover. Those missing any pages, or sections of pages, are worth 1/3-1/2 less than a complete copy.

Sports enthusiasts find that there is no substitute for the information that is found in guidebooks. A well-stocked library of sports information can be used by its owner as a constant resource. Most public libraries have nothing on their shelves to compare with what many sports collectors have in their own homes.

In 1973 and '74 press guides were issued that highlighted the accomplishments of one athlete-Hank Aaron. Press interest was so great during the months preceeding Hank's historic homer #715 that these guides became essential.

Shown is the 1951 baseball annual published by the National Baseball Congress of America. The audience for such non-professional baseball publications is small.

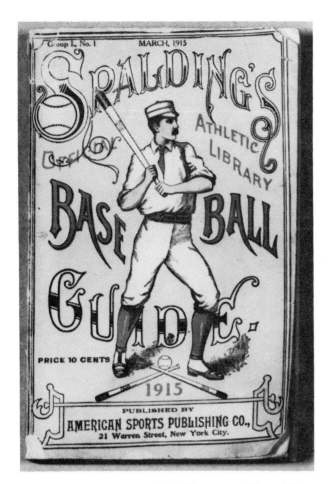

Spalding's "Official Baseball Guide" was issued from 1878 through 1939. It is one of the most popular publication series.

Baseball is the popularity king in most areas of sports collecting. The media guide is no exception. Guides issued for spring training, such as the 1960 White Sox pictured, are more difficult to obtain than the regular season books. Championship teams, such as the 1968 and '72 Tigers, are in higher demand. The Padres' 1973 guide features Nate Colbert and his 13 RBI afternoon from the '72 season on the front cover.

The Sporting News issued their baseball record book from 1909 through 1941. It's death coincides with the birth of the Guide in 1942. The record books were 3″ x5¼″ and fit into most shirt pockets. Because of this very functional format, copies in excellent condition are in short supply.

Sporting News guides have been issued annually since 1942. The book still sells for approximately $2, and is a bargain at twice that price. Previous issues now sell in a range from $3 to $15 and are, for the most part, easy to obtain.

"The Baseball Dope Book," also published by **TSN**, appeared in 1942, and from 1948 to present. The book is now used as a premium by the **Sporting News** to new subscribers. It is popular with uniform collectors as it contains player numbers.

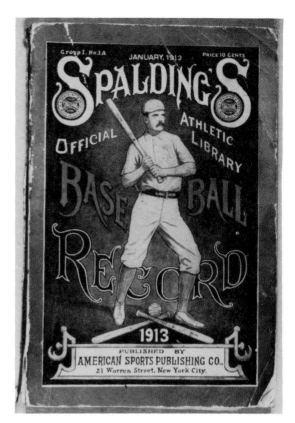

One of the most sought-after publications is this "Souvenir Record Book," sold at Comiskey Park during the 1919 World Series. The book features many player photos of the participants.

College football guides have a particular interest in certain sections of the country. Many college releases are far superior to those issued by the professional clubs in printing quality, layout, and content. Shown here are some of the better school issues. The University of Michigan, which averages close to 95,000 fans per game, is almost 'obligated' to keep its working press informed. The University of Nebraska sells its guide to Cornhusker followers, and has no problem in exhausting the supply of 2,000 issued each year. The University of Syracuse dedicated its 1973 guide to 25-year coach Ben Schwatzwalder. Eastern Michigan University sports information director John Fountain racked up another NCAA award for this 1970 guide.

The "Official Baseball Record," published by Spalding, was printed from 1908 to 1924. Though not as popular as Spalding's "Guide," it still has great collector interest.

College teams that gain notoriety through winning teams provide guides that become collectors items. Pictured are basketball guides from Memphis State's fine '72 season, UCLA's, National Championship team of 1972 (also sold to the public), and Iowa State's championship wrestling and gymnastics teams.

Art Rooney, Pittsburgh Steeler owner, is featured on the cover of this 1951 guide. Also pictured in this composite are the Lions' 1970 guide, Buffalo (1973), San Diego (1975); and the Denver Broncos' guide that was issued prior to the opening of their summer camp in 1975.

Professional football has long issued guides for the media. Shown here are publications from Pittsburgh (1947), Detroit (the uniform numbers indicate the year-1966), Chicago (commemorating the Bears' 50th year in the League), the Saints (1971), the 1972 Broncos and the 74 Packers.

The media guides that are issued for the Super Bowl employ the same cover design as the program. (See color plates in program section.)

As evidenced by this selection of professional basketball guides, many are issued as yearbooks to the general public. Those from the Pacers, Colonels, Spirits, 76'ers, and Hawks all fit into this category.

The '73-'74 Houston Aeros' guide signalled the return of hockey's greatest. The Minnesota Fighting Saints' first two guides are shown, WHA scoring champ Mike Walton is featured on the '74-'75 edition. The Chicago BlackHawks' and Toronto Toros' guides were available to the public. The cover of the Philadelphia Flyers' 1974-75 media guide tells the whole story: Stanley Cup Champions. The Cup is embossed, in solid silver, on a black background.

Hockey guides have long been a combination yearbook-press publication. The Toronto Maple Leaf book in the upper left corner was issued in 1962-63 as a pictorial review of their Cup victory, as well as guide for the media with current team information. Those issued by the Canucks, Penguins, Rangers, Canadiens and Blues were also sold to the public as yearbooks, fact books or official guides. The Blackhawks' guide pictured was solely a press issue.

The value of any collection increases when you have completed a 'run' from any one team. This set of Miami Dolphin guides begins with their first season - 1966.

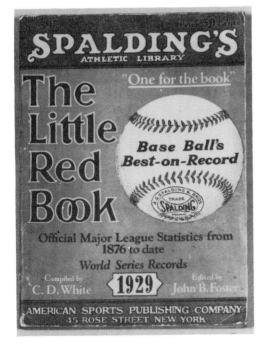

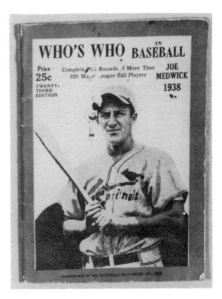

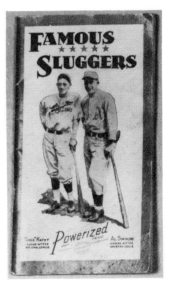

The Hillerich & Bradsby Company first issued their "Famous Slugger Yearbook" in 1921. It has been printed annually since 1927. The publication contains player photos, as well as statistical information. "The Little Red Book" was issued from 1926-1932, and again from 1934 to 1971. "Who's Who in Baseball" first appeared in 1912. After a three year absence, it has been published annually to date.

Yearbooks

Yearbooks, as we know them today, are a recent phenomena. While several baseball clubs issued pictorial publications in the 30's and early 1940's, the proliferation of what we commonly think of as yearbooks did not begin until after World War II.

Most collector interest in yearbooks is confined to the sport of baseball. With few exceptions, the issuance of yearbooks has been a baseball 'exclusive.' The Green Bay Packers have issued yearbooks for a number of years, and since 1970 other professional teams have joined the ranks of those printing them.

Yearbook values are dictated by age, condition, scarcity, demand, and sometimes by the record of the team that year. Championship teams' yearbooks are more popular than those of also-rans. Yearbooks missing pages, or with pictures cut out, have little value.

Official yearbooks, those issued by the teams themselves, have a much higher value than the 'unofficial' editions released by independent publishing houses. It is easy to distinguish these from the ones printed by the teams.

Some baseball clubs will revise their yearbooks periodically through the course of the season. These revisions include recent player transactions, and are normally indicated as a 'revised edition.' One edition usually will have a smaller distribution than the others, resulting in a higher value.

IDENTIFICATIONS OF ILLUSTRATIONS ON PAGE 33

A. 1953 Philadelphia Athletics Yearbook this unofficial edition was published by Big League Books.

B. 1955 St. Louis Cardinals Yearbook: this unofficial edition was published by Big League Books.

C. 1959 Chicago White Sox Yearbook: this official yearbook carries a higher value because of the Sox' success in '59.

D. 1961 New York Yankees Yearbook (revised): this updated edition was released by the Yanks in June of 1961. This was another of their championship years.

E. 1962 Milwaukee Braves Yearbook: this official volume is enhanced by the presence of Hank Aaron on this team, and the fact that the franchise has sinced moved to Atlanta.

F. 1968 Detroit Tigers Yearbook: this official issue has a higher demand because of the Team's 1968 World Series victory.

G. 1969 Kansas City Royals Yearbook: this official publication was issued mid-way through the Royals' first season. Initial yearbooks normally have a higher market value.

H. 1972 California Angels Scorebook: the Angels have issued a series of pictorial scorebooks in lieu of a yearbook since 1968.

I. 1973 Pittsburgh Pirates Yearbook: this club-issued publication includes a special commemorative section in tribute to the deceased Roberto Clemente. Pirate yearbooks of the 70's are among the most attractive issued.

IDENTIFICATIONS OF ILLUSTRATIONS ON PAGE 34

A. 1974 Atlanta Braves Yearbook: official Atlanta yearbooks, prior to 1975, have an increased demand because of Aaron's assault on Ruth's home run records.

B. 1974 New York Yankees Yearbook: this official yearbook also contains a detachable stereo record highlighting 50 years of Yankee history.

C. 1975 Minnesota Twins Yearbook: the cover of this official yearbook was reserved for 1974 American League batting champion Rod Carew.

D. 1975 San Francisco Giants Yearbook: the Giants' '75 attendance hit an all-time low; which may increase the value of this yearbook in future years. The book contains a section on baseball trading cards.

E. 1974 Kentucky Colonels Yearbook: this basketball yearbook is one of the only such publications that is not a combination media guide.

F. 1962 Green Bay Packer Yearbook: the Packers have issued yearbooks since 1960. Strong fan support has warranted such an illustrated publication.

G. 1972 Miami Dolphins Book: this hard bound book was released following the Dolphins' '72 Super Bowl victory. It was produced by the Miami club.

H. 1974 New Orleans Saints Yearbook: this official edition contains player profiles and highlights of the 1973 season.

I. 1968-69 Detroit Red Wing Yearbook: this yearbook features a section on Gordie Howe, as well as this cover painting of hockey's greatest performer. The pages of this publication are not numbered.

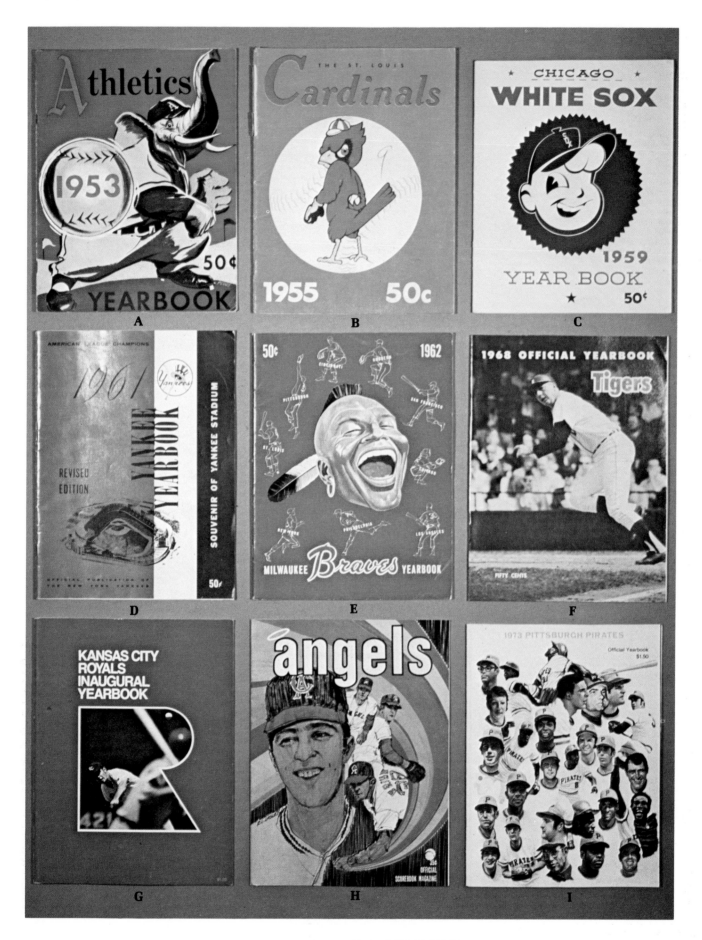

A   B   C

D   E   F

G   H   I

FOR DESCRIPTIONS, SEE PAGE 32

A   B   C

D   E   F

G   H   I

FOR DESCRIPTIONS, SEE PAGE 32

Programs

Since the 1870's, the favorite souvenir of fans attending athletic contests has been the program. The program has evolved from the functional listings of participants to the photo/ad-packed, standardized magazines of today. In between, a number of changes have been seen, not all of which are good.

The first programs were actually 'scorecards,' one piece of printed paper stock, usually folded in half to form four pages. The scorecard is almost extinct today, being used in only a few of the major league ballparks. It would be impossible to determine when the first advertisement appeared on a scorecard. Whatever that date may be, they have been with us ever since. Photos became an integral part of the program, or scorebook, in the Teens. The introduction of pictures necessitated additional pages, and with that, more advertisements. Paper shortages during War Years eliminated some programs, and caused a reduction in the number of pages in others. As computerizations may prove the eventual death of ticket collecting, standardization could very well squelch any remaining interest in program collecting.

For over 100 years each program established its own identity. The size, layout of the players' pictures, the style of type on the scoring pages, the artwork on the cover, all contributed to make each program a 'unique' souvenir. With the over-expansion of professional sports in the 1970's came the arrival of the standardized program. Professional football fans, no matter where they happen to see a game on any given Sunday, are offered programs that have the same cover picture, most feature stories, and many of the ads. In many cases these **Pro** editions differ only in the lineup pages and a few advertisements. Much is the same with **Goal,** distributed in NHL arenas; and **Hoop,** sold at NBA contests. In 1974 and '75 a universal program was used for Baseball's World Series; and in those same two years, the All-Star Game programs were sold to thousands of television viewers. The aspects that have captivated the attention of the collector may soon be gone.

The factors that dictate the values of programs are age, importance of the game that was played, attendance at that game, whether the item is scored or unscored, the players involved in the game, and most importantly — condition. A combination of these factors can result in a valuable collectible. For example, the 1942 Baseball All-Star Game played at the Polo Grounds in New York. The game was played in a war year, fewer programs than normal were printed because of paper shortages. The game was delayed for hours because of rain, so, many of the programs sold were used for seat covers, or to keep the rain off the fans' heads. A program from this game is a very fine item. Many other examples exist, and with some investigation into the circumstances surrounding sporting events you will be able to draw your own conclusions.

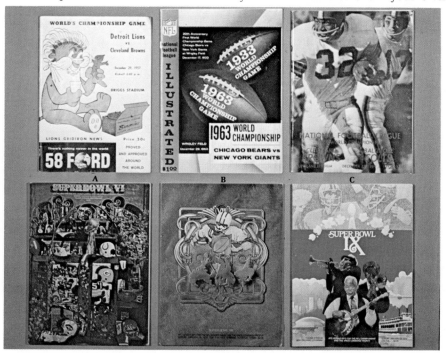

A

B

C

D

E

F

G

H

I

FOR DESCRIPTIONS, SEE PAGE 41

A

B

C

D

E

F

G

H

I

FOR DESCRIPTIONS, SEE PAGE 41

A

B

C

D

E

F

G

H

I

FOR DESCRIPTIONS SEE PAGE 42

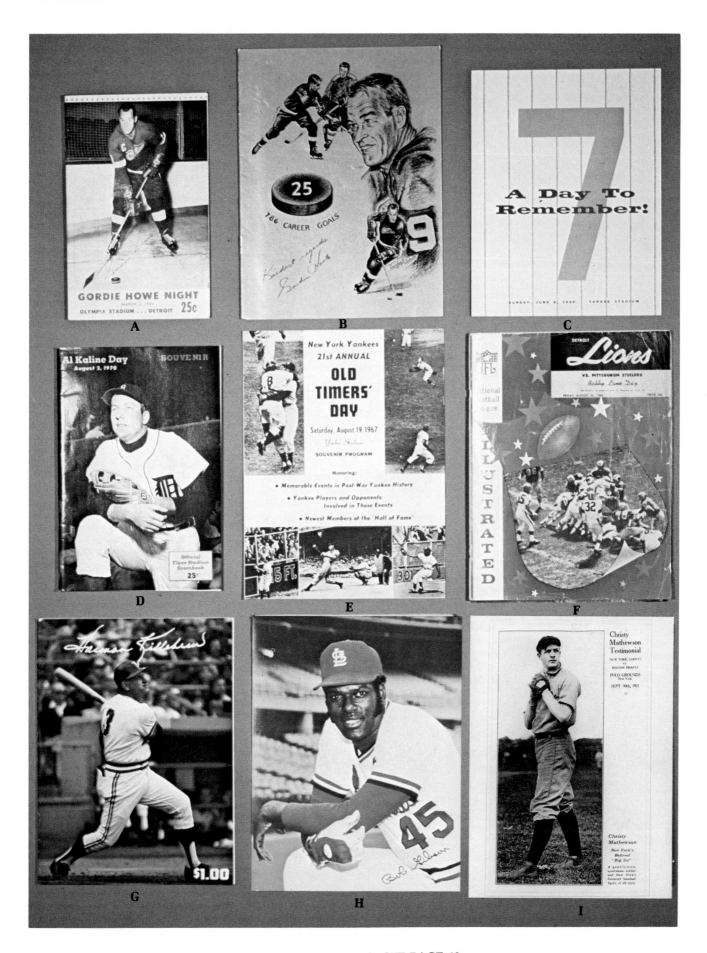

A

B

C

D

E

F

G

H

I

FOR DESCRIPTIONS, SEE PAGE 42

FOR DESCRIPTIONS, SEE PAGE 42

IDENTIFICATIONS OF ILLUSTRATIONS ON PAGE 35

Football Championship programs have a great interest among collectors. The National Football League's World's Championship games were played consecutively from 1933 to 1966. The American Football League Championship Games were staged from 1960-66. The Super Bowl was inaugurated in January, 1967 and has been played as a World's Championship Game.

A. 1957 NFL Championship at Detroit, Michigan; Lions vs. Browns.
B. 1963 NFL Championship at Chicago, Illinois; Bears vs. Giants.
C. 1964 NFL Championship at Cleveland, Ohio; Browns vs. Colts.
D. Super Bowl VI at New Orleans, LA; Cowboys vs. Dolphins, 1-16-72.
E. Super Bowl VIII at Houston, Texas; Dolphins vs. Vikings, 1-13-74.
F. Super Bowl IX at New Orleans, LA; Steelers vs. Vikings, 1-12-75.

IDENTIFICATIONS OF ILLUSTRATIONS ON PAGE 36

With the exception of 1904, the World Series has been played consecutively since 1903. Programs from these games have become important collectibles to many hobbyists. Because this is a 'Series,' there are actually two sets of programs to a complete set: one from the games held in the American League parks, the other from the National. In 1974, a universal program was issued for the Series, and sold at both parks. In addition, the program was available to thousands of television fans through a mail order offer. This new practice, like the computer ticket, may proven the eventual death of World Series program collecting.

A. 1935 Series, Detroit at Chicago.
B. 1938 Series, Yankees at Chicago.
C. 1962 Series, San Francisco at New York.
D. 1963 Series, New York at Los Angeles.
E. 1968 Series, Detroit at St. Louis.
F. 1968 Series, St. Louis at Detroit.
G. 1971 Series, Pittsburgh at Baltimore.
H. 1971 Series, Baltimore at Pittsburgh.
I. 1966 Series, Baltimore at Los Angeles.

IDENTIFICATIONS OF ILLUSTRATIONS ON PAGE 37

An All-Star Game affords the sport fan with the opportunity to see some of the greatest players, in one place, in head-to-head competition. All of the legendary players have played in the games at one time. Programs from these games represent special souvenirs to all those lucky enough to have attended them.

A. Baseball All-Star Game, 1940, St. Louis. This game has been played consecutively, with the exception of 1945, since 1933. In 1959-62, there were two games held.
B. Baseball All-Star Game, 1971, Detroit. Game was highlighted by Reggie Jackson's tremendous home run off the light tower in right-center.
C. Baseball All-Star Game, 1972, Atlanta. Aaron's homer before hometown fans becomes one of his career highlights.
D. Baseball All-Star Game, 1973, Kansas City. Johnny Bench was the top vote-getter for this classic.
E. Baseball All-Star Game, 1974, Pittsburgh. This program was available to thousands of television viewers through a mail order offer. The mail order programs have the game scored on the center pages.
F. NHL All-Star Game, 1974, Chicago. Hockey's All-Star Game has been held each year since 1947.
G. 1975 National Basketball Association All-Star Game, Phoenix. This game has been held each year since 1951.
H. 1941 College All-Star Game. This Game has been held every year, with the exception of 1974, since 1934.
I. 1974 College All-Star Game. This Game was cancelled due to the NFL Players' strike against club owners.

IDENTIFICATIONS OF ILLUSTRATIONS ON PAGE 38

Championship playoff games often provide some of the most memorable events in the world of sport. Shown on this page are programs from eight championship games, and one from the Indianapolis 500. Baseball play-off series began with the 1969 season. The WHA Avco Championship Series was first held in 1973.

A.   1969 National League Play-Off Series, New York Mets at Atlanta.
B.   1975 WHA Avco Championship Series, San Diego at Houston.
C.   1973 Stanley Cup Finals, Montreal at Chicago.
D.   1965 Stanley Cup Play-Offs, Chicago at Detroit.
E.   1972 Canada-Russia Series: this unusual program was distributed throughout Canada for the benefit of television viewers watching the four games of the Series that were played in Moscow. Re-caps of the first four games, played in Canada, are included in this booklet.
F.   1969 ABA Championship Series, Oakland at Indiana Pacers.
G.   1972 NBA Championship Series, Knicks at Lakers.
H.   1975 NBA Play-Offs, at Kansas City Kings.
I.   1963 Indianapolis 500: covers on these Race Classic programs have remained very similar from year to year.

IDENTIFICATIONS OF ILLUSTRATIONS ON PAGE 39

Special days, set aside to honor distinguished athletes, provide attractive program-souvenirs for those in attendance. On this page are pictured nine of these 'classic collectables.'

A.   Program from the first Gordie Howe Night, held in Detroit on March 3, 1959.
B.   This program was given to each person attending the second Gordie Howe Night in Detroit on March 12, 1972.
C.   This four page program was given to those attending Mickey Mantle Day in New York June 8, 1969.
D.   Program from Al Kaline Day, held August 2, 1970 in Detroit. At the cover price of 25¢, this was one of the greatest bargains in the history of memorabilia!
E.   This four page pictorial folder was given to those attending the 1967 Old-Timers Game at Yankee Stadium.
F.   Bobby Layne Day in Detroit, August 30, 1963, released this program that contained one of the classic printing errors. Apparently the printer confused Layne with Dick Lane who was a current member of the Lion team.
G.   This 32 page booklet was sold at Harmon Killebrew Day, in 1974 at Minneapolis. Lineups and scoring pages from the game played that day are not in this publication.
H.   1975 Bob Gibson Day Folder: this four-page summary of Gibson's career is highlighted by this striking cover picture.
I.   1921 Christy Mathewson Day Program: this nostalgic publication includes several pictures of Mathewson, as well as numerous poems and his complete major league records. This is truly a great sports collectable.

IDENTIFICATIONS OF ILLUSTRATIONS ON PAGE 40

A.   1942 St. Louis Browns Scorecard.
B.   1949 Chicago Cub Scorecard. Player inset on cover is Andy Pafko.
C.   1951 Chicago White Sox Program.
D.   1952 New York Baseball Giants Program.
E.   1960 New York Yankees Program.
F.   1963 Chicago White Sox Program.
G.   1974 Atlanta Braves Program. This particular program is from the game in which Aaron hit home run #715. This same cover was used throughout the season.
H.   1975 Milwaukee Brewers Program: this cover was used for the first games of the '75 season, commemorating Aaron's return to Milwaukee.
I.   1942 Pittsburgh Steelers vs. Boston Yankees Football Program.

Pictured here are four examples of programs that have a standardized basic format. Even the World Football League, that tried so desperately to appeal to its fans, utilized such a publication.

Programs from the first game played by a franchise, or the last in a stadium, have a wider collector interest, and higher value.

Programs from defunct WHA clubs are popular with an ever-increasing number of collectors.

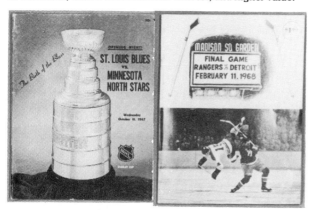 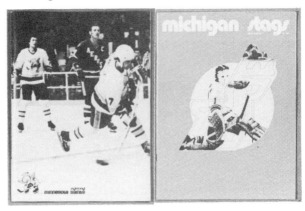

Most major PGA tournaments issue large, colorful programs. Collector interest in such events is currently low.

Older professional football programs, such as this 1927 Chicago Bear edition, are attracting the attention of more hobbyists each year.

Pictured is the program from the 1923 International Race that matched famous three-year-olds Zev and Papyrus. Collectors of horse racing memorabilia form a very small percentage of the active sports hobbyists.

Trading Cards

The trading card has been a part of American life since the early 1800's. The first of these cards were actually advertising pictures, but soon captivated the interests of a new breed of collectors. Trading cards are actually a sub-division of a larger collecting field — Paper Americana. Likewise, sports subjects comprise a small percentage of the total number of topics.

The sports trading cards span a period from 1878 to present. This 100-year continuum is divided into five significant time frames: pre-1900, 1900-1918, 1920-29, 1933-42 and 1948 to present. The cards are further separated into two major categories; National issues and Regional issues.

The vast majority of sports trading cards feature subjects from baseball, football, basketball, boxing, hockey and track and field. Baseball is the most prevelant, and is the most popular with collectors. In recent years the other sports cards have become more 'collectable.'

It is safe to say that at least 80% of all sports collectors have some involvement in the trading card division. This particular area is not only the most organized at this time, but also provides the diversity necessary for almost universal appeal.

Trading card values, like any other collectable, are dictated by supply and demand, and condition. Age is a factor, but in many cases is not a valid indicator of value. Assigning accurate condition labels to trading cards is a major point of contro- versy in the Hobby. The most acceptable categories of condition are: poor, fair, good, excellent and mint. These classifications, though, are very arbitrary. What is a 'good' condition card to one collector may be 'excellent' to another. Disputes usually occur over conditions from the middle three categories. There is usually little question over poor or mint cards. As a rule, when in doubt about exact labelling, a collector should choose the lower classification.

The major reference work on trading cards is **The American Card Catalog,** last published in 1960. The **Catalog** utilizes a complicated coding system that has been abandoned in this work. The book has not been updated in over fifteen years which means that there are countless issues that are not included. The coding system has also been a source of frustration for beginning collectors, as well as many veterans. For example, many collectors feel that most others know what an R-314 is. In actuality 75% of the hobbyists would have to refer to the **Catalog** for clarification. Most collectors do not own a copy of **The Catalog**, so, when card sets are referred to by code numbers many are often unable to identify them.

A frequently asked question among beginning collectors is, "How can I tell what year this card was issued?" Proficiency in this procedure increases as you become accustomed to the various issues. By examining the card you will be able to narrow the possibilities, and often establish exact dates.

Example 1 — You can tell from the biography on this card that the earliest possible year that it could have been released is 1937, since it mentions events that took place in the 1936 season. The biography also indicates that Bridges was purchased by the Tigers in 1930 from a minor league club and has been with Detroit ever since. The last sentence reveals that he has a nine year major league average. Beginning with 1930, a nine year period would go through the 1938 season. (This card was issued in 1939.)

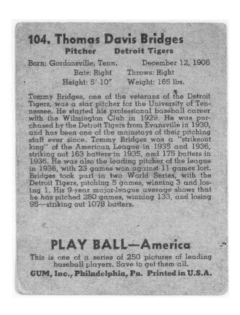

Example 2 — This specimen is a bit more difficult. The data mentions the year 1957, and accomplishments for the following year (1958). By examining the Major League Pitching Record you can see that he has played one year in the Majors (Stats for 'year' and 'life' are identical.) The earliest this card could have been released would be 1960. From the information on this card you are not definitely informed the card was issued in 1960, but the possibilities have been reduced. (This card was part of the 1960 Topps set.)

Example 3 — The biographical commentary mentions the 1961 season, and Snyder's performance. It also mentions that he came to Baltimore in 1961. The earliest printing of this card would be 1962. While the information is not sufficient to say that it was printed in 1962, again, the choices have been limited. (This card belongs in the 1962 Topps set.)

Example 4 — Cards with complete statistical records are the most easy to establish issue dates. Find the last year listed, in this case 1966, and add 1 to it. (This card is a member of the 1967 Topps edition.)

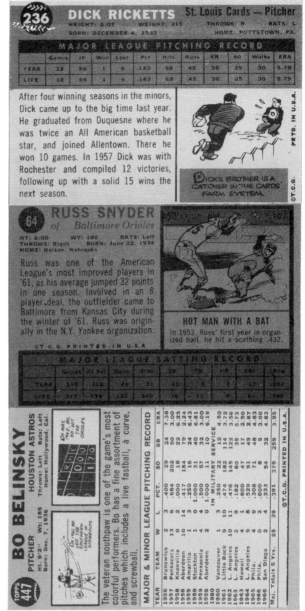

Examples 2 and 3 can often be confirmed if you have more than one sample from that same year to examine. Card designs, front and back, are normally not copied into other sets. By matching the designs on the card backs you will be separating the cards into 'years' even though you have yet to establish what that year is. From a number of samples you should be able to identify issue dates for most sets. Other helpful references would be a baseball encyclopedia, or football encyclopedia. By looking up the player's records you will learn what years he played with the team indicated on the card. Additional indicators include the copyright date, manufacturer, card number, team name and player's position.

Another aspect of card values that has affected supply and demand in recent years is the 'superstar' status assigned to certain players. It is not clear even today who is to blame for this practice — the buyer or the dealer. It's another example of the chicken and the egg paradox. Some collectors, mostly the younger, are content with acquiring just the cards of their favorite players. Dealers, seeing that their supplies of these popular players were being depleted, began to raise the prices on those cards. Cards now in this 'superstar' category — Mays, Mantle, Aaron, Ruth, Gehrig, Williams and Jackie Robinson — command often ridiculously high prices. Another group of players — Spahn, Campanella, Koufax, and Ford, to name a few — bring higher prices than the others in any particular set. Most other HOF members also have inflated price tags. Some dealers have begun to apply this practice to the stars of football — Namath, Sayers, Simpson, Jimmy Brown, etc.

National Card Issues

National issues are those that were produced in large numbers for distribution to most parts of the country. Unlike many regional cards, most National releases feature players from a wide variety of teams. Like most sports cards, they were inserted into other products as a 'bonus' to the customer.

Predominant National editions include tobacco cards, gum cards, cereal cards, and cards sold in department-type stores.

On the following pages you will find examples, and descriptions, of over 300 card sets that were distributed nationally. A few sets that were released on a regional basis are also included because of their close association with National issues of that era. In addition, a few premiums are also included due to their common labelling as a 'card' set.

Pre 1900

American tobacco producers introduced a new product to the public in the late 1800's — the machine-made paper wrapped cigarette. The primary tobacco sales had been confined to tobacco wrapped cigars, chewing cuts, and loose cuts.

In order to increase interest in their new item, many of the companies began to include small, colorful trading card inserts in the packages. The subjects on the cards included flags, boxers, coats of arms, weapons, flowers, fish, birds, fruits, actors, actresses, Indians, soldiers, wild animals, police captains and baseball players. Because there were no newsreels, or picture magazines, the cards were very 'real.' The cards of Indians, in particular, were very timely because the West was still being contested. Most of these sets included 50 cards.

The distinction of the first baseball set has been given to an 1878 issue of 13 cards by the Boston National League Club. The tobacco issues first appeared in 1886. Some of the primary tobacco producers of this era were the Kimball, Goodwin, Allen & Ginter, Duke and Lorillard Companies. Under their different brand names they began to insert these colorful cardboards in their 5¢ packages of cigarettes. These became so popular that they eventually were included in the cigar and chewing tobacco products. Most also served as a stiffener for the package itself.

Action photography was unheard of at this time, so any photographs that were used on the cards pictured posed subjects. It is easy to see that the backgrounds on many of the photos were painted drapes, that some of the 'bases' are actually pillows, and that some of the strings suspending baseballs are still visible. The long exposure time required in photography at this time necessitated this 'staging.'

This era of pre-1900 card production ended in the 1890's when most of the tobacco companies merged to form the American Tobacco Company conglomerate.

DESCRIPTIONS OF ILLUSTRATIONS ON PAGE 65

It is not precisely known how the public proceeded to acquire the albums shown on pages 65 and 66. The most logical guess would be that these were a premium release of some type. If that is the case, you may ask why they are being pictured here, instead of in the premium chapter. To answer any question that may arise, I have opted to insert them here, in full color so that you will have an opportunity to view some of the most rare, and undoubtedly some of the most beautiful, sports collectibles in existence. With all of the advancements that have been made in the last 100 years, the printing and color quality of these albums is unequalled.

A. ALLEN & GINTER ALBUM OF WORLD'S CHAMPIONS: this pictorial portfolio was released in 1887 with the first series of the Allen & Ginter tobacco cards. The album pages illustrate all of the personalities who were also issued individually with the tobacco products. The cover includes a pugilist (boxer) and a diamond participant.

B. KIMBALL CHAMPIONS OF GAMES AND SPORTS: all four of the baseball subjects in this set of 50 are shown on this page from the 1887 Kimball album. Notice that the album's binding was accomplished by stringing through the three holes on the left hand side of the page. All pages are blank on one side, providing greater quality to the illustrations.

C. OLD JUDGE BASEBALL: this unique circular album was distributed in 1889 by the Goodwin Company — manufacturers of Old Judge cigarettes. The back sides of the pictures contain the schedules for each of the teams and the records of some players. Unlike the others, the pictures used in the album are not the same as those on the cards. One hole is present for the string binding.

DESCRIPTIONS OF ILLUSTRATIONS ON PAGE 66

A. ALLEN & GINTER ALBUM OF WORLD'S CHAMPIONS: this two-page presentation reveals eight of the 50 subjects that are included in the 1887 issue.

B. OLD JUDGE BASEBALL: unlike the page featuring several New York team players (see page 65) only one member of the Boston club is pictured.

C. ALBUM OF GOODWIN'S CHAMPIONS: this bound volume was issued in 1888 and features the 50 subjects who were also released individually in the Old Judge and Gypsy Queen tobacco products. Four of the eight baseball participants are shown here.

DESCRIPTIONS OF ILLUSTRATIONS ON PAGE 67

A. 1880's OLD JUDGE BASEBALL: there are literally thousands of different cards in this set that was issued between 1886-90. Some of the cards are numbered, are a very thick cardboard, and were issued by the Goodwin Tobacco Company in their Old Judge Cigarette products.

B. 1890's S.F. HESS ATHLETES: the exact number of cards in this issue is still a mystery. The cards were released by the S.F. Hess Tobacco Company of Rochester, N.Y. in their product line.

C. 1887 OLD JUDGE NEW YORK N.L. BASEBALL: the format of this Goodwin Company release is quite different than those of the same era in that drawings are used rather than photographs. Eleven cards are known in this set.

D. 1888 GYPSY QUEEN: Gypsy Queen was another brand name in the Goodwin Company's product line.

E. 1887 BUCHNER LEADERS: there are over 300 personalities pictured in this early set. To date, there are 142 known baseball subjects. The balance of the set is composed of ship captains, policemen, jockeys and actors. The set was distributed by the D. Buchner Company of New York City. The cards, like almost all other issues of this period, are unnumbered.

F. 1888 ALLEN & GINTER'S WORLD'S CHAMPIONS (Second Series): the same 50 subjects that were issued in a smaller version are included in this set. The player's card from the smaller set is found against a larger background. These larger cards are more scarce than the common size of this era.

G. 1887 ALLEN & GINTER'S WORLD'S CHAMPIONS: there are 10 baseball subjects in this set of 50. (See pages 65 and 66 for album and more set details.)

H. 1895 MAYO'S CUT PLUG BASEBALL: there are forty different players pictured in this set. Some of the players in this set are pictured in street clothes. There are eight players which are listed with two team affiliations; bringing to 48 the total variations. The cards are not numbered. They were issued by the P.H. Mayo Company of Richmond, VA.

I. 1889 NUMBER 7 CIGARS: only eight cards are known in this set. The pictures are black line drawings, and are unnumbered. The cards were most likely distributed in boxes of cigars.

J. 1888 GOODWIN'S CHAMPIONS: there are 50 subjects in this set, eight of them baseball performers. (See page 66 for album and additional set information.)

K. 1887 KIMBALL'S CHAMPIONS OF GAMES AND SPORTS: there are 50 personalities pictured in this set, four of them baseball subjects. (See page 65 for album and additional set information.)

L. 1890's NEWSBOYS LEAGUE BASEBALL: the exact number in this set has yet to be determined. The cards were distributed by the S.F. Hess Tobacco Company in their product packages. This is a novelty issue in which paperboys are illustrated in baseball uniforms.

M. 1893 YUM YUM PAPER PICTURE CARDS: there are 28 different known 'cards' in this set. The pictures are actually coupons. There are 10 known sports drawings, and the card pictured is the only baseball.

N. 1887 FOUR BASE HITS: only six cards as known in this set. They were distributed with Four Base Hits brand cigarettes, a product of the Charles Gross Company.

O. OLD JUDGE CABINET PHOTO: these would technically be classified as a premium issue by many collectors; but, most consider them to be 'cards.' Many different poses exist, with new discoveries being made each year. Issued by Goodwin with Old Judge and Dog's Head tobacco. Over 260 known cards.

P. 1895 NEWSBOY ACTRESSES AND BALLPLAYERS: eight baseball subjects are known in this set which also contains entertainment personalities. The cabinet photos are numbered. Additional cards will most likely be found in future years.

Q. 1887 KALAMAZOO BATS: issued by the Gross Company, there are 48 known cards in this set. Some cards picture more than one player and six team photos have been seen. Cabinet-size team photos also exist, but only four have been checklisted.

R. 1890's TALK OF THE DIAMOND: this set of 25 baseball comics was distributed with products of the Duke Company of Durham, N.C. and New York City. No actual players are illustrated.

1900 — 1916

The second major period of card production occurred during the years 1900 through 1916. The major portion of these issues were distributed as inserts in tobacco products.

The tobacco companies began to use colorful trading cards as an addition to one of their new products — Turkish cigarettes. It was thought that these popular cards of the 1800's would boost sales. They were right. Hundreds of different series featuring dancers, Indians, puzzles, actors, animals, Spanish American War scenes, great explorers, flags, college pennants, boxers and baseball players were inserted into such brands as Hassan, Mecca, Fatima, Turkish Trophies and Turkey Red. In order to compete with the new smoking fad, other companies began to issue the cards in their regular cigarette products, chewing tobacco and cigars.

Almost as popular as the cards themselves were the cloth blankets, silks with pictures, leather items and buttons that were often inserted into the packs as an added 'bonus.' Many of the companies also offered large pictures, blankets or silks that were available by redeeming a certain number of tobacco wrappers or coupons.

The cards were popular with the smoker, and his family. To capitalize on the interests of the younger, non-smoker, candy and gum companies began to include cards with their products. Caramel candy was the bubble gum of the pre-1920 era. Prominent in this distribution were the American Caramel Company, Colgan's Gum, Williams Caramel and Cracker Jack. In addition, other businesses such as bakeries, clothing stores and magazines released editions.

This era came to an end with the commencement of World War I. Paper supplies were short, and many of the dyes that had been used in the production of the cards had been imported from Germany. The War made it virtually impossible to continue their printings.

DESCRIPTIONS OF ILLUSTRATIONS ON PAGE 68

A. 1912 HASSAN TRIPLE FOLDERS: this unique set of cards has 76 different center sections. There are 144 different end panel players that when combined with the centers form 132 total cards in the issue. The end panel pictures are actually reproductions of the 1911 Gold Bordered tobacco issue. The cards are not numbered, and were distributed with Hassan cork tip cigarettes.

B. 1910 RAMLY AND T.T.T. TOBACCO BASEBALL: there are 121 known subjects in this set. The cards are not numbered.

C. 1913 FATIMA TEAM PHOTOS: each of the 16 baseball teams are pictured in this set, distributed by the Liggett & Myers Tobacco Co. of Virginia. The public could obtain a 13 x 21 enlargement of the smaller card by sending 40 Fatima coupons to the Company. Both St. Louis Teams are considered scarce and command top prices.

D. 1911 MECCA DOUBLE FOLDERS: two players are pictured on each of 50 different cards. The cards are hinged, and by lifting the top panel up (just below Street's mitt) a longer (4 ¾") picture of Walter Johnson appears. Both players' drawings utilize the same feet and ground area. Both players' 1910 statistics are found on the card backs.

E. 1909-10 WHITE-BORDERED BASEBALL SERIES (T-206's): although sixty plus years have passed since this set was issued, they are still relatively available. The reason for their plentiful supply is that they were distributed in every package of tobacco by 16 different brands. Unlike cards issued with other products such as gum, caramel or cereal; the numbers of people purchasing the tobacco products was far greater. There are 523 different player poses known in this set (3). A general breakdown can be made into three categories: major leaguers, minor leaguers (2), and Southern League (also minor league) players. Included in this set is the Hobby's most legendary collectable — **the** Honus Wagner card (1). This card, of which there are less than 20 in existence, has been sold for as much as $1,500. The Wagner card is certainly not the rarest sports card, but the numerous folk stories that are constantly used to explain its scarcity has caused it to rise to the top of most collectors' want lists. Another reason is that the wide popularity of this set has increased the number of hobbyists who are attempting to complete their sets. The cards of Eddie Plank, Demmitt, St. L. Amer.; and O'Hara, St. L. Nat. are also very difficult to locate.

F. 1913 FATIMA FAMOUS PERSONALITIES: there are 54 known subjects in this set which includes individuals from baseball, entertainment and track and field.

G. 1911 SERIES OF CHAMPIONS: there are 24 known cards in this set, four of them are baseball performers. The cards are unnumbered, and were issued with two tobacco brands.

H. 1911 GOLD-BORDERED BASEBALL SERIES (T-205's): there are over 200 known player poses and variations in this set. There are 12 minor league players pictured, and these are considerably less plentiful than the major league players. This series was released by ten different cigarette brands, most of which were also involved in the 1909-10 white-bordered cards. The front formats are different for each of the two major leagues. National League players' cards include facsimile autographs (1). Players from the American League contain a bat and ball decoration (2) and the name printed out.

I. 1912 BROWN BACKGROUND BASEBALL SERIES: this set was distributed with five different brands of tobacco products. The cards are not numbered. The card of Loudermilk of the Cardinals is uncommon. Several other cards demand slightly higher values.

J. 1909-11 OBAK BASEBALL: this set was issued on the West Coast, and includes players from the Pacific Coast League and the Northwest League. There are 426 different players pictured in what is actually three different series. Four variations exist, making the total of 430. The cards were released by Obak mouthpiece cigarettes.

K. 1910 OLD MILL BASEBALL: there are 560 players in this issue, which was released in eight separate series. Each of the series were distributed only in the areas in which the players performed; ie. Texas League players issued only in the cities that had League franchises. The cards are not numbered, and contain no statistical information. The cards have distinctive red borders.

L. 1910 RED SUN BASEBALL: there are 75 players in this set, which was released by the Red Sun Cigarette Company. The cards feature players from the Southern League and are not numbered. The photos in this issue are identical to those of the previous Old Mill issue and have colorful green borders.

M. 1910 CONTENTA BASEBALL (B&W): there are 213 known players in this black and white photo series of players from the Virginia, Carolina and Eastern Carolina Leagues. The cards are unnumbered.

N. 1909 CONTENTA BASEBALL (Colored): there are 16 players pictured from the Virginia, Eastern Carolina and Carolina Leagues. It was issued prior to the version described in 'M.'

O. 1909 WORLD'S CHAMPION ATHLETES: there are 50 cards in this set of famous athletes. The cards are not numbered, and were distributed in packages of Pan Handle Scrap chewing tobacco.

P. 1911 BASEBALL SILKS: these fabric reproductions of the gold-bordered cards of the same year were found as inserts in the tobacco products. Like the blankets, many people would sew numbers of these into larger cloth items such as pillow cases, doilies, doll blankets, etc.

Q. 1910-11 SERIES OF CHAMPION ATHLETES AND PRIZEFIGHTERS: evidence on the card back indicates that a portion of the cards in this set were issued in 1910. Other cards have statistical data that is comprehensive through 1910. There are 153 known cards which include boxers, track and field, golfers, bowlers, aviators and billiards players. They are not numbered, although some cards are marked "Series #2, 51 to 100."

R. 1911 PINKERTON BASEBALL CABINETS: these large photo cards are anonymous, but are thought to be distributed by the Pinkerton Tobacco Company. The cards are numbered.

DESCRIPTIONS OF ILLUSTRATIONS ON PAGE 69

A. 1910 PROMINENT BASEBALL PLAYERS AND ATHLETES (T-3's): few sets can match this one for color, or collector appeal. The set is technically a premium issue. Most collectors, though, consider this a card issue. There are 126 subjects pictured, including 26 boxers. The pictures were obtained by redeeming coupons from cigarette tobacco. Recent increased interest in this set has driven prices up drastically.

B. 1911 SPORTING LIFE BASEBALL: there are 288 cards in this set, distributed through the **Sporting Life** magazine. The set is composed of twelve different cards from each of 24 different teams. The publications' readers could order a packet of a particular team by sending a coupon and 4¢. The complete set sold for 96¢. This complete set is quite valuable today. Several subtle photo variations are known.

C. 1909-1910 AMERICAN CARAMELS BASEBALL, Type One: there are 119 known pictures in this, one of the first of the candy issues. The cards are not numbered.

D. 1910 BASEBALL GUM: this set of 50 different player poses was distributed by the Croft & Allen, Dockman and Nadja companies. The cards are unnumbered, and similar in appearance to the set described in 'C.'

E. 1902 PROMINENT BASEBALL PLAYERS: this set of player poses features black and white photo fronts, and the wording "One of one hundred and fifty prominent baseball players" on the reverse side. A few are also known with blank backs. The cards were distributed by the Breisch, Williams Company. To date, there are 147 known cards in the set, including several players that appear on two different teams.

F. 1910 BRIGGS BALL PLAYERS: there are 30 different players in this set, two with two team designations, making the total 32. The cards were distributed by the C.A. Briggs Co.

G. 1910 AMERICAN CARAMELS BASEBALL, Type Two: this is a set of 11 members of the Pittsburgh Pirates. The lettering on the card fronts is blue, rather than the black on the larger set of 119. The backs are identical. They are not numbered.

H. 1908-10 AMERICAN CARAMELS BASEBALL STARS: there are actually three separate sets using the same photos that have been placed under this general heading. The first issue of 33 cards lists teams on the backs in the order Athletics, New York and Chicago; and, was issued in '08. The second issue of 33 cards, issued the following year, lists teams as Chicago, Athletics and New York. The third, and last, set issued in 1910 lists teams as Pittsburgh, Washington and Boston.

I. 1910 WILLIAMS CARAMEL BASEBALL: this set of 30 different players is blank-backed, and unnumbered. Each player's portrait is surrounded by a red background.

J. 1911 GENERAL BAKING COMPANY BASEBALL: although this is technically a regional issue, most collectors consider it compatible with the early caramel cards. There are 25 players in this set. The cards were distributed with bread labelled Buster Brown, Family, Brunners, Butter-Krust and Peerless brands.

K. 1911 ROCHESTER BAKING WORLD CHAMPIONSHIP SERIES: this set utilizes the same format as the Nadja Play Ball Baseball issue of the same year. This set was distributed by the Rochester Baking Company, and includes members of the victorious 1910 Philadelphia Athletics' team. The card fronts also include the wording "World Champions" and, the elephant symbol was added to the players' uniforms. Because of these similarities, most experts group this issue with the early candy cards.

L. 1910 TIP-TOP BREAD BASEBALL: this set highlights 25 Pittsburgh Pirate team officials and players. Unlike most cards of this era, it is numbered, 1-25.

M. 1910 PLOW BOY BASEBALL PHOTOS: this set is devoted to players from each of the two Chicago baseball clubs. At present, a total of 38 different are known. The cards came in large tins, or 'lunch boxes' as they were called, of tobacco. A relatively recent discovery, the set is gaining in popularity among collectors.

N. 1909-13 COLGAN'S CHIPS BASEBALL DISCS: these unique, circular discs were issued with Colgan's Violet Chip and Mint Chip chewing gum. The gum pieces themselves were round, thin slices.

O. 1914 BASEBALL BLANKETS (B-18's): these felt squares, inserted into various brands of cigarette tobaccos, were a very popular item of their time. Consumers would sew the squares into large blankets; hence the term 'blankets.' There are nine players issued for each of ten teams. However, each player has two variations of background coloring, bringing the total to 180. In addition, there are seven other variations, making the set complete at 187.

P. 1910 JU JU DRUMS BASEBALL DISCS: there are 32 known players pictured in this set; very similar to the Colgan's issue.

DESCRIPTIONS OF ILLUSTRATIONS ON PAGE 70

A. 1912 INTERNATIONAL LEAGUE BASEBALL PLAYERS: there are 90 players pictured in this set. The cards are numbered.

B. 1916 SPORTING NEWS BASEBALL: this set is complete at 200 cards. The cards were obtained on a premium-type basis. This numbered set is similar to those issued by Weil, Globe Suits, and numerous other firms.

C. 1910 AMERICAN CARAMEL DIE-CUT BASEBALL: the card backs contain a checklist for players available from the same team. The only teams that have been reported are Pittsburgh, Boston, A.L., Philadelphia A.L. and N.Y., N.L. The checklist is numbered, although the individual cards are not. It is anticipated that cards were issued for each team.

D. 1916 BOSTON STORE BASEBALL: there are 200 different numbers in this set. These cards from the Chicago-based store are very similar to the set issued by the Weil Baking Company of Louisiana and Collins-McCarthy candy of San Francisco. The only difference is the card's back.

E. 1914-15 CRACKER JACK BASEBALL: this set features players from the American, National and Federal Leagues. In 1914, the series included 144 cards. The 1915 set utilized the original 144 players, and an additional 32 for a total of 176. The cards are numbered, and were found inside boxes of the favorite caramel pop corn.

V. 1911 PLOW'S CANDY BASEBALL: there are 35 known players in this large-size issue. Note the similarities in card color, and format to the Plow Boy Tobacco cards issued at approximately the same time. Chances are good that these cards were found in tin boxes of candy.

1920 — 1929

The third significant era of trading card production was 1920-1929. The beginning of this period was marked by the end of the first World War; the end, by the Great Depression.

The major printers of trading cards in this decade were the candy and gum companies, and companies who produced the cards for sale in department-type stores. Popular in this prior category were the 'strip' cards. Eight to ten cards were sold in a strip. Some were given to purchasers of certain candy products. Most were cut by scissors into individual cards.

Significant card producers in this period were the American Caramel Company, Oxford Confectioners, National Caramel Company, International Feature Service, to name a few.

By 1929, with the country in its worst economic turmoil, most retail sales had trailed off. The public, scrambling to stay alive, turned its attention to things other than candy and strip cards.

DESCRIPTIONS OF ILLUSTRATIONS ON PAGE 70

F. 1922 AMERICAN CARAMEL BASEBALL PLAYERS: there are 240 subjects in this unnumbered set with the unusual ornate borders. The American League players are sepia, on a light yellow stock; and the National pictures are printed in a dark green ink.

G. 1922 OXFORD CONFECTION BASEBALL: twenty players are included on the checklist that appears on the card backs. The cards are unnumbered.

H. 1920's GAME CARD: this sample is typical of several playing card games that were issued during this period.

I. 1920 BASEBALL DRAWINGS: there are 120 numbers in this set. The card number is found on the card fronts. One of the many anonymous issues of this era.

J. 1920's STRIP CARD: there are several anonymous issues that were released in strips of 4-8 cards. By tearing along a perforated section, the strips became individual cards. This set was issued with all red ink, all black, or red and black. The sets include personalities from baseball, boxing, aviation and the entertainment field.

K. 1921-22 AMERICAN CARAMEL BASEBALL SERIES: this issue is actually composed of two sub-sets, one of 80 cards, the other of 120. From most indications, these cards were released throughout the ten years of the Century's second decade. The cards are not numbered.

L. 1920's NATIONAL CARAMEL BASEBALL SERIES: this set of 110 cards was probably issued in more than one year. This series could easily be confused with the issue described in 'K' without discerning the card backs. The cards are not numbered.

M. 1923 WILLARD'S CHOCOLATES BASEBALL: there are 175 unnumbered cards in this set, which was issued and distributed in Canada.

N. 1922 BROOKLYN BASEBALL PHOTOS: there are 16 photos in this anonymous issue. The cards are numbered 101-116. A team picture appears, along with 15 individual shots. Similar sets are known for other teams.

O. 1926 PERSONALITIES DRAWINGS: this set of 50 sketches includes ten baseball performers, and 40 personalities from boxing, aviation, etc. The cards are numbered 1-50.

P. 1924 CU&U BASEBALL DRAWINGS: this set of 60 diamond personalities is numbered, and contains the trademark 'CU&U.' (Underwood & Underwood)

Q. 1922-24 CIFS BASEBALL PHOTOS: there are 101 known cards in this unnumbered set. This strip card set includes the trademark 'CIFS.' (International Feature Service)

R. 1926 PERSONALITIES DRAWINGS (Second Series): this set is actually a second series of the issue described in 'O.' There is a slight change in format, leading to the original classification as a separate issue. The cards are numbered 51-100.

S. 1920's CIFS BASEBALL DRAWINGS: there are 30 players pictured in this numbered set. The trademark 'CIFS' appears on the cards.

T. 1920's STRIP CARD: see description of 'J' for details.

U. 1920's SFIC BASEBALL DRAWINGS: this set is actually a variation of the CIFS set described in 'S.' More color differentials exist in this version, with the trademark spelled backwards, 'SFIC.'

W. 1921 YORK CARAMEL BASEBALL: there are 60 numbered cards in this black and white set.

1933 — 1941

The fourth general interval for the production of trading cards was 1933-41. There are a few isolated issues that were released prior to 1933 and after 1929; and some after 1941, but, the vast majority of these editions came out after the Depression, and ended with the U.S.' involvement in World War II.

The major characteristics of the majority of these issues is the fact that they are larger in size compared to the tobacco and early caramel cards; the cardboard is usually thicker, and almost all were distributed with chewing gum.

The significant card producers in this era were the Goudey Gum Company of Boston, the National Chicle Company of Cambridge, Mass., Gum Incorporated of Philadelphia and the U.S. Caramel Company. These companies, and others, released colorful trading card pictures of Indians, aviators, movie stars, presidents, football and baseball players. The most popular were the heroes of the diamond.

Most of the gum cards were sold in waxed paper packages that included three cards and a slab of chewing gum. They sold for 1¢. In addition to large photos of favorite ballplayers, the public was also able to redeem the wrappers for rings, medals, buttons and pins.

Cards from this period are now in high demand, while the supply is relatively low in comparison to the earlier tobacco issues. The paper drives during the War eliminated thousands of these cards. The demand is heightened by the fact that some of baseball's greatest performers appear on cards in this time period. Collectors wishing to add cards of Babe Ruth, Lou Gehrig, Dizzy Dean, Mickey Cochrane or Mel Ott usually find them in these editions. The first major football set was produced in 1935 and includes some of the Game's greatest players.

The extreme paper shortages that began in late 1941 as America stepped up its role in the Second World War signalled the end of the card printings until 1948.

DESCRIPTIONS OF ILLUSTRATIONS ON PAGE 71

A. 1933 GOUDEY BASEBALL: the most popular set of the 30's or 40's, there are 240 cards in the complete set. The interest in this set is fueled by the fact that there are four different Babe Ruth cards, and one of the rarest sports cards of any era, #106, Nap Lajoie. The Lajoie card was not issued in 1933. As the legend goes, so many collectors wrote to the Goudey Co. that in 1934 they issued the card and sent one to the complaining parties. This card has recently sold for as much as $500.

B. 1933 GOUDEY SPORTS KINGS: this set of 48 cards includes performers from a variety of different sports. There are three baseball stars (Ruth, Cobb and Hubbell), four boxers, and three swimmers, to mention a few.

C. 1933 U.S. CARAMEL FAMOUS ATHLETES: this set, primarily baseball stars, is composed of 32 cards. The set's popularity is enhanced by the presence of both Ruth and Gehrig.

D. 1934 GOUDEY BASEBALL: there are 96 cards in this colorful set. The set can be easily recognized by the "Lou Gehrig Says" logo that appears across the card bottom of most cards. Eleven cards use the "Chuck Klein Says" variation (left). The most sought after card in the set is #37, Gehrig. Most collectors feel this is the finest picture of Lou in any card edition.

E. 1935 GOUDEY PUZZLE CARDS: there are 36 different front panels, each picturing four different players, in this set. The backs, when pieced together, form large pictures. There are many different backs known for the basic 36 fronts.

F. 1936 GOUDEY BASEBALL: there are 25 different card fronts in this set. The card backs are used to play a baseball game, and each card exists with as many as seven different backs. The cards are black and white, and are not numbered.

G. 1938 GOUDEY HEADS-UP BASEBALL: this set exists in two versions; the Foxx card pictured on the left with a clear background, and with comments and cartoon characters such as the DiMaggio card on the right. The same 24 players are pictured in each version. The plain background cards are numbered 241-264, and the cartooned are labeled 265-288.

H. 1941 GOUDEY BASEBALL: there are 33 different players featured in this set. Each player, though, was issued with a red, yellow, blue or green background.

I. 1934-36 NATIONAL CHICLE DIAMOND STARS: there are 108 different players in this set that was issued, and reissued over a three year period. Cards numbered 97-108 are more difficult to find and usually sell for twice the price of the lower numbers.

J. 1935 NATIONAL CHICLE FOOTBALL: one of the only football sets issued prior to the post World War II era, it is complete at 36 cards. Cards numbered 25-36 command a slightly higher price than the first 24 numbers. The set includes Rockne, Nagurski, Ken Strong and Cliff Battles.

K. 1933 TATOO ORBIT BASEBALL: there are 60 players in this set. The cards are unnumbered, and feature black and white head shots with red and yellow backgrounds.

L. 1933 DELONG BASEBALL: this issue of 24 players is the hardest set of the 30's issues to complete. A complete set, in excellent condition, has a catalog value of over $500. The cards had limited distribution in comparison with the Goudey's and Diamond Stars.

M. 1934-36 NATIONAL CHICLE BATTER-UPS: this set of 192 different poses was issued over a three year period. The cards are die cut around the player's picture so that when punched out, they form a stand-up figure. The card number is contained on the front, as the backs are blank. Numbers 81-192 are more difficult to obtain, and have a higher value. Most of these cards found today have been punched out, decreasing their value.

N. 1939 PLAY BALL BASEBALL: there are 161 cards in this set, numbered 1-162. Card #126 was not issued. The card fronts are black and white photos, and contain no lettering.

O. 1940 PLAY BALL BASEBALL: there are 240 different players pictured in this set. The Gum, Inc. manufacturer added the player's name to the card front as an improvement to the 1939 issue. Card numbers 181-240 bring a higher market price.

P. 1941 PLAY BALL BASEBALL: eleven members of the HOF are included in this set of 72 cards. This is the most popular of the Play Ball issues because of the colorful format that was used.

Q. 1941 DOUBLE PLAY BASEBALL: there are 75 cards in this set, with two numbers and players per card. The card fronts were printed with brown ink on a white paper stock. These cards are often seen cut into individual cards, decreasing the value.

DESCRIPTIONS OF ILLUSTRATIONS ON PAGE 72

A. 1933 BUTTER CREAM CONFECTIONARY BASEBALL: there are 29 different players known in this set. The cards are unnumbered, and now contain twelve Hall of Fame members.

B. 1932 SEPIA BASEBALL SERIES: there are 54, numbered cards in this set. The manufacturer is not known.

C. 1943 M.P. & COMPANY BASEBALL: there are 24 known players in this strip card set. The cards are numbered 100-124. Several numbers have yet to be identified.

D. 1935 GOUDEY KNOT-HOLE BASEBALL GAME: there are 24 cards in this baseball game. No individual player's photos appear in this set. The cards are numbered.

E. 1933 GEORGE C. MILLER BASEBALL: there are 32 unnumbered cards in this set. Players from both leagues are featured. The set's popularity is increased by the fact that it contains 18 Hall of Fame performers.

F. 1930 RITTENHOUSE CANDY BASEBALL: a different player's profile is included in the center of each of the 52 different cards in a standard deck. The card backs contain one letter from the Rittenhouse name: R-I-T-E-N-H-O-U and S. Prizes were awarded to those spelling the manufacturer's name.

G. 1930's SCHUTTER-JOHNSON MAJOR LEAGUE SECRETS: it is believed that this set of drawings is complete at 50 cards, although many have yet to be found. The cards include the commentary of a famous player of the era explaining how he accomplishes a certain feat. The cards are numbered.

H. 1935-41 WHEATIES SPORTS PANELS: the Wheaties cereal box sports panels became an 'institution' in American life. The most popular breakfast cereal of the time would regularly introduce new personalities to the public. The public was able to read of the career exploits of their sports heroes at the kitchen table by reading the product's box.

I. BASEBALL CARD WRAPPERS: while no monetary value has been placed on the package wrappers from sports cards; there is no doubt that very few of these exist today. Youngsters were too concerned about getting at the contents of the gum and cards to worry about the wrapper. Some collectors prize their accumulations of these colorful waxed papers. (1)-1935 Goudey "Big League" contained the Four-In-One puzzle cards. (2)-1935 Goudey "Sports Kings" held the cards of the same name. (3)-1937 "Big League" contained the Knot-Hole game cards. (4) "Diamond Stars" held three cards of the same name and a piece of gum. The packs all sold for a penny.

1948 — 1976

The fifth major grouping of trading cards begins in 1948, and continues to the present. The end of World War II signalled the resumption in the production of trading cards. Paper was no longer in short supply, and several gum companies were anxious to reinstitute the successful business aspects used by Goudey and National Chicle prior to 1942.

The major manufacturers involved in card printings in the late 40's were the Leaf Company and the Bowman Company. Leaf printed its last card set in 1949; attributed to a legal hassle with Bowman over the rights to use certain player's photos. The Topps Company of Brooklyn, N.Y. and Duryea, Pennsylvania printed its first major sets in 1951. For the next four years they were involved in a great marketing, as well as legal, battle with Bowman. In 1956, Topps purchased the Bowman Company.

Other companies that have issued significant sets of sports trading cards during these years include the Fleer Company of Philadelphia, the Post Cereal Company with three 200-card sets, the Parkhurst Company of Canada (primarily hockey cards), the Philadelphia Gum Company, and recently the Kellogg's Cereal Company with their three-dimensional baseball sets.

Topps has remained the 'king' of this industry for over twenty years. In 1975, Topps printed 250 million baseball cards. Baseball is the biggest sports issue they produce, but not their best seller. Elvis Presley, Batman, Monkees and Wacky Packs all have been more popular in the years they were released in comparison to the baseball edition of that year. Another 250 million sports cards are divided between hockey, basketball and football. Football cards are much more acceptable with today's youth than they were twenty years ago — evidenced by the size of the sets, now over 500 cards.

DESCRIPTIONS OF ILLUSTRATIONS ON PAGE 73

A. 1948 LEAF BASEBALL: Leaf's legal disputes with the Bowman Company caused many of the numbers in this set to be either removed prior to release, or soon after. Over 80 cards have been seen, some in very scarce quantity. The cards are numbered. Some cards carry a 1949 copyright date.

B. 1948 SPORT THRILLS: this set, issued with Swell Gum, illustrates great moments in the history of baseball. There are 20 cards in the set. The wrappers were redeemable for a Bob Feller button.

C. 1948 BOWMAN BASEBALL: The Bowman Company's answer to the Leaf issue was this 48 card black and white set. The cards are numbered.

D. 1948 LEAF FOOTBALL: this unique printing accomplishment features black and white flesh areas, with color painted on to the other areas. There are 98 cards in this numbered set.

E. 1948 BOWMAN FOOTBALL: there are 108 numbered, black and white cards in this set. Many different premium offers were outlined on the card backs.

F. 1948 LEAF BOXING: there are 49 known cards in this set. The cards are skip-numbered, and an album offer claims that it can display 168 different Knock-Out cards.

G. 1948 BOWMAN BASKETBALL: Bowman's first color release was this 72 card basketball series. The popularity of basketball cards must have been dealt a blow by this issue as ten years passed before there was another round-ball release.

H. 1949 BOWMAN BASEBALL: there are 240 players, plus a few variations, in this set. The card fronts appear with (1), and without (2) the player's name. Cards numbered 200-240 are particularly difficult to obtain.

I. 1950 BOWMAN BASEBALL: there are 252 cards in this full-color set. Cards from the first series are slightly harder to locate. At this time, the Bowman Company had a 'curb' on the market. Their monopoly would not last long.

J. 1950 BOWMAN FOOTBALL: the color quality in this set was far superior to the previous Bowman releases. There are 144 cards in the set, numbered.

K. 1950 ROYAL STARS OF BASEBALL: there are 24 numbered cards in this set. The cards were printed on the back panels of Royal Gelatin. It is difficult to find even a sample card from this set, today.

L. 1951 BOWMAN BASEBALL: Bowman adopted this larger format, and player identification on the card fronts in this set of 324 cards. This was the largest of all the Bowman issues. Cards numbered 253-324 are in limited supply.

M. 1951 TOPPS BASEBALL: the Topps Company entered the hobby card market with two 52 card sets, one with red and white backs, the other blue and white. (The Company had issued some sets the previous year on a test basis.) The cards were distributed, two to a package, with caramel candy. Perforations divided the two cards.

N. 1951 BERK-ROSS "HIT PARADE OF CHAMPIONS": sold in packets of 18, nine panels of two, in department/toy stores by the Berk-Ross manufacturer. The set includes 72 cards, or four different folders of 18. Performers from all sports are pictured.

O. 1951 BOWMAN FOOTBALL: the format of this Bowman issue was very similar to their baseball set of a few months earlier. There are 144 cards in a complete set.

P. 1951 TOPPS MAGIC FOOTBALL: this was the first major football issue by the Topps Co. A year earlier they released a set of very small felt college football pennants. This '51 set features 75 of the country's finest collegiate players. A silver 'scratch-off' panel covered the answers to a football quiz.

Q. 1952 TOPPS BASEBALL: the Topps Company adopted this larger format to gain an 'upper hand' on Bowman. This set is very difficult to complete, as cards numbered 311-407 are in scarce supply. This last series also happens to contain some of the bigger stars of the day in Jackie Robinson, Eddie Mathews, Roy Campanella and Mickey Mantle. The Mantle card, in excellent condition, regularly sells for more than $50.

R. 1952 BOWMAN BASEBALL: this set of 252 cards utilizes the player's autograph on the card front for identification. Numbers over 216 command higher prices.

S. 1952 RED MAN BASEBALL: the Pinkerton Tobacco Company issued a set of 52 cards with its Red Man chewing tobacco in 1952 and 1953. In 1954 and '55, the sets were reduced to 50 in number. The cards all have a coupon, redeemable for a baseball cap. The year and the number appear on this 'tab.' You can also distinguish the year by subtracting one from the date of expiration on the premium offer. The cards have a higher value with the coupon intact. The same drawing was used for players appearing in the set more than one year, with alterations made to the background.

T. 1952 BERK-ROSS BASEBALL: there are 72 players pictured in this set, which like the 1951 B-R issue, was sold in dime stores. There are two poses of Phil Rizzuto. The cards are not numbered, and include partial records from the 1951 season.

U. 1952 BOWMAN FOOTBALL: two identical sets of 144 cards each were released. One set (2) is larger than the other (1). No rationale has yet to be formulated explaining this occurrence. The set utilizes the Bowman picture/painting method.

V. 1953 BOWMAN BASEBALL (Colored): a nation-wide poll of collectors in 1974 made this issue a landslide winner as the most popular set. There are 160 cards in the set. The player's picture is the only thing on the card fronts.

W. 1953 BOWMAN BASEBALL (Black & White): in an attempt to offset the popularity of the Topps issue, Bowman released this 64-card set late in the summer. It apparently was not very popular, as there are comparatively few of these cards in supply today.

X. 1953 TOPPS BASEBALL: although the cards are numbered to 280, there were only 274 issued in this set. Numbers 253, 261, 267, 268, 271 and 275 were not released. It is thought now that this was a ploy on the part of Topps to increase sales to those seriously attempting to complete the set. The pictures are actually paintings of the players, and have always been popular with the men pictured.

Y. 1953 TOPPS RINGSIDE: this set of 96 featured famous wrestlers and boxers. Card number 48 is particularly scarce. The cards were printed two cards to a strip with perforations.

Z. 1953 BOWMAN FOOTBALL: there are 96 cards in this set. Even though Bowman was the only manufacturer of football cards at the time, the result is this somewhat small set.

AA. 1953 PARKHURST HOCKEY: this set, printed and distributed in Canada, contains 105 cards. This was Parkhurst's second set, after a successful initial effort in 1952.

DESCRIPTIONS OF ILLUSTRATIONS ON PAGE 74

A. 1954 TOPPS BASEBALL: there are 250 numbered cards in this set. Topps introduced the format of including an action shot in accompaniment with the player's profile in this issue. There are two cards, 1,250, of Ted Williams.

B. 1954 BOWMAN BASEBALL: this set is complete at 224 cards. Player names are identified on the card fronts by either autographs, or printed. Card number 66 appears as Ted Williams or Jimmy Piersall. The Williams card is one of the most difficult post WW II cards to acquire. Apparently Ted's picture was released, and later removed. It is interesting to examine the possibilities of this situation in light of the fact that he is on two of the Topps cards this same year. Piersall is also #210 in this set.

C. 1954 RED HEART DOG FOOD: there is no question that this 33 card set was one of the most colorful, and well produced, sets of all time. The cards are unnumbered. There are eleven green, blue, and red cards.

D. 1954 PARKHURST HOCKEY: there are 100 players in this set from the Toronto, Detroit and Montreal teams.

E. 1954 BOWMAN FOOTBALL: the cards in this set are numbered 1-128. The color quality of these cards is very good.

F. 1950-56 CALLAHAN HALL OF FAME SKETCHES: this set, depending on the year of issue, varied in size from 60-80 cards. The cards were sold in a set, boxed, at Cooperstown.

G. 1954 QUAKER SPORTS ODDITIES: this 27 card set describes strange events in a wide variety of sports. The cards were distributed in boxes of Quaker cereal.

H. 1954 TOPPS LOOK 'N' SEE: this card of Babe Ruth is the only sports performer pictured in a set that includes great historical personalities.

I. 1955 TOPPS BASEBALL: the numbers in this set run through 210, although there are only 206 cards. Numbers 175, 186, 203 and 209 were not printed. Last series cards, 161-210, are more difficult to find.

J. 1955 BOWMAN BASEBALL: this was the last baseball set issued by Bowman. It is the only modern set that includes cards of the umpires. This set, called 'television sets' by many, is complete at 320. Several variations exist, and these bring slightly higher prices.

K. 1955 TOPPS HOCKEY: this was the first Topps hockey set, and is complete at 60 cards. The cards picture players from the four U.S. teams in the NHL.

L. 1955 TOPPS DOUBLE HEADERS: this set is patterned after the 1911 Mecca issue. There are 66 cards, each portraying two players. By lifting up the flap on the card front, another player's sketch, longer in size, will appear. Both players have common feet and ground section.

M. 1955 BOWMAN FOOTBALL: this set of 160 cards was the Bowman Company's last sports issue. Background colors on these cards are very brilliant.

N. 1955 TOPPS FOOTBALL: the Topps Co. resumed production of football cards with this set of 100 all-time great college players.

O. 1956 TOPPS FOOTBALL: this set is complete at 120 cards. Topps reign as the only NFL football card producer began with this issue, and lasted through the 1959 season.

P. 1956 TOPPS BASEBALL: this set is complete at 340 cards. Several team cards, the first to appear in a set since the 1951 issue, appear with the year '1955' added to the team's identification. There are also two unnumbered checklist cards.

Q. 1957 TOPPS BASEBALL: this set (2) is complete at 407 cards. In addition, there are four unnumbered checklists (1). The first Topps checklists were issued with the 1956 issue. In the 1958 issue, the checklists are found on the back of the team cards. In 1961, they became a separate, numbered part of the sets. Cards numbered 264-352 in this '57 set are more difficult to obtain. No explanation has yet been given for the scarcity of this series, which was neither the first nor last series of the issue. This is the first Topps issue that features complete, year-by-year, player statistics on the backs.

R. 1957 TOPPS FOOTBALL: this set includes 154 cards. The fronts include both a head, and action, shot.

S. 1958 TOPPS BASKETBALL: the Topps Company's first basketball release included 80 cards. The set was obviously not very popular with youngsters, as Topps did not issue another until 1970.

T. 1958 TOPPS BASEBALL: this set is complete at 494 cards. This was Topps' largest set to date. The special All-Star cards were introduced by Topps in this issue. They have been a part of most sets since. Stan Musial appears on a Topps issue for the first time, also. Card #145 was not issued.

U. 1958 TOPPS FOOTBALL: in 1958, Topps began printing the Canadien, as well as the American, football cards. The only differentiating aspect of the first few sets is the player's team. The Canadien cities belong in the foreign issue. The American set includes 132 cards, the Canadien 88.

V. 1957 TOPPS SCOOPS: this set includes accounts of great events in the course of history; several of them from the world of sports.

W. 1958 TOPPS HOCKEY: this was Topps' second hockey issue, and included 66 cards of players from the four U.S. teams.

X. 1958 HIRES ROOT BEER: this set of 66 cards was distributed with Hires soft drink products. The cards were issued with a detachable coupon across the bottom. The cards are numbered 10-76. A test set, with solid-colored backgrounds, was issued prior to this one.

DESCRIPTIONS OF ILLUSTRATIONS, ON PAGE 75

A. 1959 TOPPS BASEBALL: includes a total of 572 cards. This is the first year that the special rookie All-Star cards were issued. Cards numbered 507-572 comprise the last series, and are in limited supply. The last series includes the All-Star selections for both leagues. Card fronts contain facsimile autographs.

B. 1959 FLEER TED WILLIAMS: this unusual set of 80 cards illustrates the life of Boston Red Sox outfielder Ted Williams. This is the first of the releases by the Fleer Gum Company of Philadelphia. Card number 68 was withdrawn just before distribution, and then later released very late in the summer. That card is one of the most difficult of all post WW II issues to locate. The 79 other cards have a composite value of $4-$5; #68 is worth 2-3 times that.

C. 1959 TOPPS FOOTBALL (American and Canadien): there were 176 cards in the American set, 88 in the Canadien. Canadien players can be differentiated by referring to the player's team—they will list such cities as Calgary, Winnepeg, Edmonton, etc. Card backs contain a rub-off quiz.

D. 1959 TOPPS HOCKEY: set is complete at 66 cards. Players pictured are from the four American teams—Detroit, Chicago, New York and Boston.

E. 1959 PARKHURST HOCKEY: there are 50 cards in the complete set. All pictures feature Montreal Canadien and Toronto Maple Leaf Players.

F. 1959 BAZOOKA BASEBALL: this is one of the most popular of all Bazooka issues—found as the under panel on boxes of penny bubblegum—as only one player is pictured. Cards are scarce in relation to other cards of this era. Complete at 23 cards.

G. 1960 TOPPS BASEBALL: can usually be distinguished by the fact that the cards are horizontal—Topps' last baseball set issued this way. The managers appear again in this set, and are vertical, as well as the pictures being sketches rather than photos. The coaches of each team appear on one card. World Series highlight cards were issued for the first time. This set, unlike the 1959 set, does not include complete year-by-year player statistics on the backs. Not again until the 1971 issue is this facet eliminated. The set is complete at 572 cards, and numbers 507-572, the last series, have a slightly higher value.

H. 1960 BAZOOKA BASEBALL: this set, found on Bazooka Gum boxes, is very similar to those issued in 1961 and '62. Each panel contains three players. There are twelve different boxes. Panels cut into single cards are less valuable than complete strips.

I. 1960 CANADIEN FOOTBALL: there are 88 cards in the complete set. The fronts differ from the American set in design, but the backs utilize the same format and green color.

J. 1961 NU CARDS FOOTBALL: this set, featuring college players, is very scarce in relation to the Topps and Fleer issues of the same year. The set is complete at 80 cards, and is numbered 101-180.

K. 1960 TOPPS FOOTBALL: 132 cards are included in this set. The backs contain a rub-off quiz.

L. 1960 FLEER ALL-TIME GREATS: this set is very popular among autograph collectors because of the many Hall of Famers included. This was Fleer's second venture into the trading card market. There are 79 cards, but card number 80, Pepper Martin, exists only as the back to one of the 79 fronts. Apparently Fleer was forced to remove Martin's picture from the set.

M. 1960 TOPPS HOCKEY: The Topps Co. continued its 66 card set-size in 1960. (The '58 through '64 sets all contain 66 cards.) All players pictured are from the Black Hawks, Rangers and Bruins.

N. 1960 FLEER AFL FOOTBALL: the new American Football League found an eager promoter in the Fleer Co. when they agreed to produce this 132 card set. Few kids, or serious collectors, knew much about the players pictured, but surprisingly, the cards were well-received, as evidenced by the relatively large supply of this issue that can be found today. The players are silhouetted against plain backgrounds.

O. 1961 TOPPS BASEBALL: Topps continued to enlarge its sets, this year to 587 cards. Cards numbered 471-486 picture the MVP's from 1950-60, and cards 401-410 feature great moments in baseball history. This is the first baseball set that includes a separate checklist card which is a part (numbered) of the complete set. Previous issues used the reverse side of team cards, or an unnumbered insert card. The 61's last series, numbered 507-589, is difficult to complete, and includes the All-Star selections. Card #589, Warren Spahn, is mislabelled and is actually the 587th card. Cards #587 and #588 do not exist.

P. 1961 FLEER ALL-TIME GREATS: the response to the previous year's set prompted the Fleer people to enlarge the 1961 edition of diamond greats to 154. This set is even more a favorite with autograph collectors. There are still, to this date, future Hall of Famers in this set. The second series (numbers 89-154) had limited distribution, and is worth 3-4 times the value of the first 88 numbers.

Q. 1961 POST BASEBALL: this unique set of 200 players, was found on the back panels of various Post Cereal products. Collectors could order 160 of this year's cards from the Post Co. These cards were also on the boxes. The other 40 cards could only be found on the box panels. Ordered cards can be differentiated from the product cards by their thickness, and the fact that they have perforation marks.

R. 1961 TOPPS FOOTBALL: Topps largest set, to that time, included 198 cards. Cards numbered 1-132 pictured the NFL players, and the later numbers the AFL. The American League players are less abundant than the earlier numbers.

S. 1961 PARKHURST HOCKEY: there were 61 cards in this Canadien issue; picturing players from Detroit, Montreal and Toronto.

T. 1961 FLEER FOOTBALL: the Fleer set this year surpassed Topps in number-220. The set features players from both leagues, and the format is radically different from the 1960 issue, or any of the Topps issues. Many of the pictures were taken in Yankee Stadium (NFL), as evidenced by the prominent architechture in most of the backgrounds. Most of the players are 'doing something' in the pictures. The AFL cards are less abundant. The cards are grouped alphabetically by team, i.e. Chicago Bears 1-9, etc.

U. 1961 GOLDEN PRESS HALL OF FAME: this 33 card set was available in dime stores and other department—type stores in book form. The cards were die cut, and 'punched' out of their original pages. The book sold for 29¢. Today, the set, in its original book form, is worth at least 20 times that.

V. 1961 CANADIEN FOOTBALL: there are 132 cards in this set. The card fronts feature black and white photos and facsimile autographs.

W. 1961 TOPPS HOCKEY: this 66 card set also features several old-timers cards such as Georges Vezina. Three American teams are again pictured.

DESCRIPTIONS OF ILLUSTRATIONS ON PAGE 76

A. 1961 SPORTS SCOOPS: there are 80 cards in this set, numbered 401-480. The card number appears on both the card front and back.

B. 1960 SPORTS NOVELTIES: this set is complete at 144 cards (2). Included in this set is the very scarce card of Jim Grant (1). Grant was originally issued with the picture of Brooks Lawrence. Late in the season, the corrected Grant (1) picture was substituted. Cards numbered 73-144 are very hard to locate. This set, issued with marbles, was produced by the Leaf Co.

C. 1962 TOPPS BASEBALL: there are 598 cards in this issue. A very popular aspect of this set is a series of 10 cards on the life of Babe Ruth. Several variation cards exist in the second series of this issue.

D. 1962 CANADIEN FOOTBALL: there are 169 cards in this small-size set. Team cards are also included, with checklists on those backs.

E. 1962 POST BASEBALL: this set is complete at 200. The cards were found on the back panels of Post breakfast cereals. The care one took in cutting them off the boxes now has a great degree of importance to their present value. Cards cut unevenly can be considered 'poor' even though the greater percentage of the card may be in excellent shape. Cards of Mickey Mantle and Roger Maris were also printed on a paper stock and distributed in magazines, as well as in super markets on tear-off pads.

F. 1962 TOPPS FOOTBALL: there are 176 cards in this black-bordered set. Some of the players' pictures are actually drawings.

G. 1962 POST FOOTBALL: this Post cereal set is complete at 200 cards. The cards are grouped in the order of the teams' 1961 season standings, i.e. Green Bay, New York, etc.

H. 1962 FLEER FOOTBALL: this Fleer set featured only players from the American Football League, and included 88 cards.

I. 1962 PARKHURST HOCKEY: there are 51 cards in this set which features players from the Detroit, Montreal and Toronto teams. The card number appears on the card fronts.

J. 1962 TOPPS HOCKEY: there are 66 cards in this set. All are members of the Bruins, Rangers and Black Hawks.

K. 1962 FLEER BASKETBALL: this set is complete at 66 cards. The first 44 cards are individual player photos. The last 22 are action shots of stars pictured in the first section.

L. 1963 TOPPS BASEBALL: the cards in this set are numbered 1-576. Several printing variations exist on a number of cards.

M. 1963 FLEER BASEBALL: this set is numbered 1-66, and has an unnumbered checklist card. Card #46, Joe Adcock, is difficult to find. This set was issued with cookies, in packages similar to the gum cards.

N. 1963 FLEER FOOTBALL: there are 88 cards in this AFL set.

O. 1963 BAZOOKA BASEBALL: there are twelve different panels, each picturing three players, in this set. The cards were found on the bottom panel of boxes of Bazooka chewing gum.

P. 1963 TOPPS HOCKEY: there are 66 hockey players pictured in this issue. The players are from the Boston, Chicago and New York teams.

Q. 1963 POST BASEBALL: this set is complete at 200. Cards were included on boxes of Post's cereal. This set, like the '62 issue, could be obtained only by purchasing the breakfast food products.

R. 1963 JELLO BASEBALL: the same 200 players that appear in the Post set are in this issue. The Jello cards are slightly smaller, and the yellow background in the statistic area is a brighter yellow. The Jello cards are more difficult to find because there was only one card to a box; as opposed to an average of eight on the cereal boxes.

S. 1963 PARKHURST HOCKEY: there are 54 cards in this Canadien issue. In addition, there is an unnumbered checklist card.

T. 1963 TOPPS FOOTBALL: this set is complete at 170. The set includes players from the National Football League.

U. 1963 POST CANADIEN FOOTBALL: this Post cereal issue features players from the Canadien Football League. It was possible to obtain some of the cards by writing to the Company.

V. 1963 BAZOOKA ALL-TIME GREATS: this set of 41 baseball immortals was an insert in boxes of Bazooka chewing gum. The cards are numbered.

W. 1964 TOPPS GIANTS: this postcard-sized set of 60 cards has a strange history. From information found on the card backs, they were not released until after the mid-season All-Star Game. Seven of the players' career recaps refer to events that took place during the 1964 season. Most collectors cannot recall ever seeing this issue in retail outlets. Today, it is one of the most common, and least expensive, sets being sold by card dealers.

X. 1964 TOPPS BASEBALL: this set is complete at 587 cards. There are no scarce cards in this issue.

Y. 1964 TOPPS STAND-UPS: this set of 76 cards is die cut so that each card can be made three-dimensional. This set's supply is very limited in comparison with the regular Topps issue of 1964.

DESCRIPTIONS OF ILLUSTRATIONS ON PAGE 77

A. 1964 PARKHURST HOCKEY: this set features players from the two Canadien teams and the Detroit Red Wings. An American flag is the background for the Red Wing players, and the British Union Jack for the Toronto players. The Montreal player cards utilize a striped background.

B. 1964 TOPPS FOOTBALL: this set includes 176 players from the American Football League. This is the first of four consecutive editions in which the Topps Co. released only the AFL cards.

C. 1964 TOPPS HOCKEY: like most of the early Topps hockey issues, this set contains 66 cards. The cards feature players from the Boston, Chicago and New York teams.

D. 1964 PHILADELPHIA GUM FOOTBALL: this is the first of four editions released by the Philadelphia Gum Company that feature players from the NFL. All of the sets are complete at 198 cards.

E. 1965 TOPPS HOCKEY: the Topps Company began production of both the American and Canadien hockey cards with this set of 110 cards.

F. 1965 TOPPS BASEBALL: there are 598 cards in this printing. No scarce, or rare, cards exist.

G. 1965 PHILADELPHIA GUM FOOTBALL: there are 198 National Football League players and team cards in this issue.

H. 1965 TOPPS FOOTBALL: this unique, large-sized card is part of 176 in this AFL release.

I. 1965 TOPPS EMBOSSED BASEBALL: this set was an insert in the Topps regular baseball issue of this year. The cards are numbered on the backs. The player's silhouette is embossed in gold on a red background for the National League, and blue for the American League. There are 72 cards in the set.

J. 1966 TOPPS FOOTBALL: there are 132 AFL cards in this 'television' set.

K. 1966 PHILADELPHIA GUM FOOTBALL: there are 198 NFL performers in this edition.

L. 1966 TOPPS BASEBALL: this set is complete at 598 cards. The backs, like most Topps issues since 1957, include complete annual player statistics.

M. 1969-70 BAZOOKA BASEBALL 'EXTRAS': this Bazooka edition was released for two years. The smaller cards (1) were found on the end panels of the box, and the larger newspaper-format cards were the back panels (2). There are 12 different numbered backs, and 30 different unnumbered end panels.

N. 1967 TOPPS BASEBALL: there are 609 cards in this set; one of the most difficult of the newer issues to complete. Cards numbered 534-607 are very hard to find. A few printing variations also exist.

O. 1968 TOPPS BASEBALL: there are 598 cards in this set. No scarcities exist.

P. 1967 TOPPS FOOTBALL: there are 132 cards in this set, the last year that Topps did not print all of the football cards.

Q. 1968 TOPPS GAME CARDS: this set of 33 playing cards was an insert in the Topps regular issue of the same year. Most of the star players are pictured.

R. 1969 TEAM CEREAL BASEBALL: this set of 24 was found on the back panels of Nabisco's Team cereal. The cards were printed on three different back panels, each containing eight players. They are not numbered.

S. 1967 PHILADELPHIA GUM FOOTBALL: this set, the last of the Philly issues, is complete at 198.

T. 1968 TOPPS FOOTBALL: this set is complete at 219. The cards of the Packers and Raides have a different background, and are horizontal.

U. 1968 TOPPS HOCKEY: this set is complete at 132 cards. This same set was also printed and distributed in Canada. It features players from all six teams, and special All-Star team cards.

V. 1968 ALL-TIME BASEBALL TEAM: this set features 14 players, plus a numbered checklist. The set was manufactured by Sports Memorabilia of Lowell, Mass.

W. 1969 TOPPS & O-PEE-CHEE HOCKEY: there are 132 cards in the American issue, and 198 in the Canadien set. The Canadien issue was produced by the O-Pee-Chee Co., a Canadien affiliate of the Topps Company. This release includes the players from the expansion teams.

X. 1969 TOPPS BASEBALL: there are 664 cards in this set. Two cards, Clendenon and Dalrymple, exist in two different versions. Cards in the last series are slightly more difficult to locate.

DESCRIPTIONS OF ILLUSTRATIONS ON PAGE 78

A. 1969 TOPPS FOOTBALL INSERTS: this set of 33 cards was a bonus in the packages of 1969 Topps football cards. Numbered, 1-33.

B. 1969 TOPPS DECKLE EDGE: this set of 35 cards is numbered 1-33. Two cards exist for numbers 11 and 22. The more scarce versions are Joe Foy and Jim Wynn. The cards were inserted into packs of '69 Topps baseball.

C. 1969 TOPPS FOOTBALL: this set is complete at 263 cards. The white bordering does not exist on the first 132 cards.

D. 1970 KELLOGG'S 3-D BASEBALL: there are 75 cards, in this the first of the three-dimensional sets. The cards were produced by the Xograph Co. and were available in Kellogg's products, as well as in dime stores. It was possible to send to Kellogg's for the entire set, keeping its present value down.

E. 1970 TOPPS BASKETBALL: this was Topps' first basketball issue since 1958, and included 99 cards.

F. 1970 KELLOGG'S 3-D FOOTBALL: there are 60 cards in this set produced by Xograph. Complete sets were available through mail-order to Kellogg's.

G. 1970 FLEER WORLD SERIES: there are 66 numbered cards in this set. Fleer's inability to mention active players by name results in interesting descriptions. Mickey Lolich is referred to as "the Tigers' lefty hero," and Yastrzemski is identified as "The Red Sox outfielder who had won the triple crown."

H. 1970 TOPPS BASEBALL: there are 720 cards in this set, Topps' largest to that date. No scarce cards exist, although last series cards are somewhat more difficult to locate.

I. 1970 TOPPS SUPER FOOTBALL: this set is complete at 35 cards. The card backs are identical to the format used in the Topps regular football issue. The cards were sold three to a pack, with a stick of gum for 10¢.

J. 1970 & 1971 TOPPS SUPER BASEBALL: the Topps Company issued these large-sized sets in both 1970 and 1971. The card backs utilize the same layout as in their regular issues of those years. There are 42 cards in the '70 set, 63 in 1971.

K. 1970 TOPPS FOOTBALL: this set is complete at 263 cards. There are no rarities.

L. 1970 TOPPS & O-PEE-CHEE HOCKEY: cards numbered 1-132 were issued in the U.S., and numbers 133-231 in Canada. Both sets feature players that are not common to the other. The Canadien series does not include #195, has two cards labeled 214, and an unnumbered card of Gordie Howe.

M. 1971 TOPPS BASEBALL: this set is complete at 752 cards (2). The Topps' Canadien affiliate, O-Pee-Chee issues baseball sets in the various Provinces. These Canadien cards, (1), can be identified by examining their backs. Most will include biographical information in both English and French, and the 'OPC' copyright. The first O-Pee-Chee baseball set was issued in 1965.

N. 1971 KELLOGG'S 3-D FOOTBALL: there are 60 cards in this set. Unlike the 1970 set, this set was not sold through an offer described on the box. The only way a set could be completed was to accumulate them one at a time by buying the cereal. The value of this set is much higher than the previous issues.

O. 1971 KELLOGG'S 3-D BASEBALL: this set is complete at 75. Because this set, too, was not available except by buying the breakfast food, its value has zoomed to the $100 plateau. The card backs exist with or without the 1970 copyright line.

P. 1971 TOPPS FOOTBALL: this set is comprised of 263 cards.

Q. 1971 DAD'S HOCKEY: there are 144 players pictured in this edition. The cards are not numbered, and each player is pictured wearing an NHL Players' Association jersey. The set was issued in Canada with Dad's chocolate cookie bars.

R. 1971 MILK DUDS BASEBALL: there are 70 known players in this set. The card numbers appear on the box end panel. If the picture is cut from the box, the number is then detached. Cards on full, uncut boxes have a higher value.

S. 1971 TOPPS & O-PEE-CHEE HOCKEY: cards numbered 1-132 were issued by Topps, and numbers 133-264 by O-Pee-Chee in Canada.

T. 1971 TOPPS BASKETBALL: there are 175 cards in this set. Apparently, the 1970 basketball set was popular with youngsters as this set is almost double in size.

U. 1971 O-PEE-CHEE CANADIEN FOOTBALL: the front design is similar to the Topps issue, and includes 132 cards. The backs have purple and black type.

V. 1971 FLEER WORLD SERIES: this set, another drawn by artist Bob Laughlin, included 68 cards. Two additional cards to the 1970 set were created by adding the re-cap of the 1970 Series, and an explanation of why no series was held in 1904. The year is in a square box, and includes the logo of the Major League Baseball Promotion Corp.

DESCRIPTIONS OF ILLUSTRATIONS ON PAGE 79

A. 1970 ROLD GOLD/KELLOGG'S 3-D ALL-TIME GREATS: this set of 15 baseball immortals was issued, one to a package, in Rold Gold pretzels. The package carried an offer to purchase the entire set. The copyright date was switched, and this set was distributed with Kellogg's Danish-Go-Rounds in 1972.

B. 1972 TOPPS & O-PEE-CHEE HOCKEY: the first 132 cards in this set were issued by Topps in America, and cards 133-264 by O-Pee-Chee in Canada. This second series includes two special collectors cards honoring Gordie Howe and Jean Beliveau.

C. 1972 O-PEE-CHEE CANADIEN FOOTBALL: there are 132 cards in this foreign set.

D. 1972 TOPPS BASKETBALL: this set of 233 is divided into two series. The first 144 cards picture NBA players, the last 89 performers from the ABA.

E. 1972 KELLOGG'S 3-D BASEBALL: there are 54 cards in this set of three-dimensional pictures. Late in the season these cards were available to the public in set-form. This set has the highest value of any of the 3-D sets that were offered to customers through mail order.

F. 1972 FLEER FAMOUS FEATS: there are 40 cards in this set, drawn by Bob Laughlin. The cards are numbered on both the front and back.

G. 1972 TOPPS BASEBALL: this set is complete at 787 cards, Topps' largest set. Cards from the last series, numbered 644-787, are more difficult to find. This is the first year Topps added the boyhood photo cards of the players to the set, and also action pictures in addition to the player profiles.

H. 1972 HARLEM GLOBETROTTERS BASKETBALL: this set of 84 cards was issued in 1972 by the Fleer Company, and a year later in Cocoa Puffs cereal. Each player is shown in many different poses through-out the set.

I. 1972 TOPPS FOOTBALL: this set is complete with 351 cards. Cards from the third series, numbered 264-351, are very difficult to locate. These usually bring a price five times that of cards from the first two series.

J. 1973 TOPPS BASEBALL: there are 684 cards in this set. The pictures are numbered 1-660, and there are also 24 unnumbered team checklist cards. This was the last set of baseball cards that Topps issued in series, over a period of 4-5 months. An interesting aspect of this set is the run of eight cards depicting all-time leaders in home runs, RBI's, victories, etc.

K. 1973 KELLOGG'S 2-D BASEBALL: this set, a drastic change in format to the previous Kellogg 3-D sets, was advertised as two-dimensional. The entire 54 card set was available by writing to the Company.

L. 1973 TOPPS & O-PEE-CHEE HOCKEY: the American Topps set is complete at 176 cards. The O-Pee-Chee Canadien edition includes 341 numbered cards. Two different checklist cards exist for #334. In addition, there is a series of 28 unnumbered cards that features the NHL performers from the Canada-Russia Series. Card #208 was not issued.

M. 1973 TOPPS FOOTBALL: there are 528 cards in this Topps Co. issue. This was the largest football issue to date, and is an indication of the ever-increasing popularity of the sport.

N. 1973 TOPPS BASKETBALL: this set is complete at 264 cards. The first 176 cards picture NBA players; the remaining 88 American Basketball Association personalities.

O. 1973 NABISCO PRO FACES: this set, distributed with Sugar Daddies candy, is complete at twenty-five cards. The cards highlight performers from football, hockey and basketball. The card backs have an adhesive coating so that they can be affixed to a large poster, available by writing the Company.

P. 1973 QUAKER OATS HOCKEY: ten panels of five cards each combine to make the 50 card set. The panels were available in Quaker products in Canada.

Q. 1973 FLEER FOOTBALL HOF: this unnumbered set included 50 cards. The set was produced by Fleer in conjunction with the Football Hall of Fame. The set has since been expanded to include a total of 84 players, and is sold at the Canton, Ohio attraction.

R. 1973 TOPPS CANDY LIDS: there are 55 discs in this Topps' test set. The lids were found on 10¢ cups of colored bubble gum nuggets.

S. 1974 WONDER BREAD FOOTBALL: there are thirty cards in this set. The fronts are very similar to the 1971 Topps issue. Topps produced this set for Wonder Bread products. The backs include a 'How To' series of football fundamentals.

T. 1974 O-PEE-CHEE HOCKEY: there are 264 cards in this Canadien issue. The first 132 cards in the set have red borders, the remaining 132 utilize green bordering.

U. 1974 TOPPS BASKETBALL: this set includes 264 cards. The first 176 cards picture NBA players, the remaining 88 ABA performers.

V. 1974 TOPPS HANK AARON CARD: this special card was issued as #1 in the 1974 Topps regular baseball issue. Topps was reasonably certain Hank would get the two homers he needed to surpass Ruth on the all-time list. In years to come, this will be one of the most sought after cards of this modern era.

DESCRIPTIONS OF ILLUSTRATIONS ON PAGE 80

A. 1974 TOPPS BASEBALL: years from now collectors will still be talking about the '74 Topps baseball set. No modern set contains more errors, variations, and unusual aspects. The set includes a special six card tribute to Hank Aaron (1). All of the Aaron cards from previous sets are pictured, four to a card, on cards 2-6. Because the O-Pee-Chee Canadien cards include both English and French translations, six of the Aaron cards contain only two previous card reproductions (2). The total number of special Aaron cards in the Canadien release is 9. Rumor was heavy in December of 1973 that the San Diego Padres would move their franchise to Washington, D.C. The first cards off the press included these 'Washington, National League' cards (4). These were later corrected to read 'San Diego' (3). There are fifteen cards that appear in both versions. This set includes 660 numbered cards, 24 unnumbered team checklists, and 44 cards in a 'traded' set. In addition, several other variations exist for certain cards. This is the first year that Topps issued the entire set at once, rather than in several series.

B. 1974 TOPPS HOCKEY: this set is complete at a 198 cards. Unlike the Canadien issue of this year, the bordering on the card fronts is not confined to green and red.

C. 1974 FLEER WILDEST DAYS AND PLAYS: this Laughlin/Fleer issue features 42 comic drawings of unusual happenings in the history of baseball. Instances such as the White Sox scoring 11 runs in one inning, on one hit; a batter running to third instead of to first on a single, and a batter being hit by pitches five times in one game are a few of the events described.

D. 1974 TOPPS FOOTBALL: this set is complete at 528 cards.

E. 1974 KELLOGG'S 3-D BASEBALL: there are 54 three-dimensional cards in this set. The complete set was available for purchase by writing the Company.

F. 1975 O-PEE-CHEE HOCKEY: this Canadien release includes 396 cards. All of the players are from the National Hockey League. The team card backs include checklists of the players from that team. There are 264 cards in the American Topps edition.

G. 1975 O-PEE-CHEE WHA HOCKEY: this test set of 66 cards was available in limited areas in Canada. This is the first hockey card set that features only World Hockey Association players. Card #1 pictures all three playing Howes.

H. 1975 FLEER PIONEERS OF BASEBALL: this 28 card set highlights great players from the formative years of the game. This, like the Fleer issues of 1973 and '74, was distributed as a bonus in purchases of gum and cloth team emblems.

I. 1975 TOPPS BASEBALL: the 1975 Topps edition includes 660 numbered cards (3). In addition, a smaller 'mini' set of 660 cards was issued as a test set in selected areas of the country (2). Topps celebrated its 25th year of baseball card production by issuing a special 24 card sequence that shows the MVP's from each year in miniature form (1). The unnumbered team checklists that were a part of the 1973 and '74 sets were incorporated on the backs of the team cards in this set. The managers, instead of appearing on individual cards, are included in an inset circle on the team card fronts.

J. 1975 KELLOGG'S 3-D BASEBALL: there are 57 cards in this, the sixth Kellogg baseball set. The complete set was made available to the public. Hunter exists with Oakland or New York team identification.

K. 1975 HOSTESS BASEBALL: this set of 150 cards was produced by the Topps Company for the Continental Baking Company, manufacturers of Hostess products. The cards are usually seen in a panel containing three pictures (1). The numbers run consecutively, so, by obtaining the 50 different panels you would complete the set. In some areas of the country individual cards were printed on the bottom packaging stiffener of single Twinkies, Cupcakes and Snowballs (2).

All photos in the following 16-page section are shown at approximately 40% of their original size.

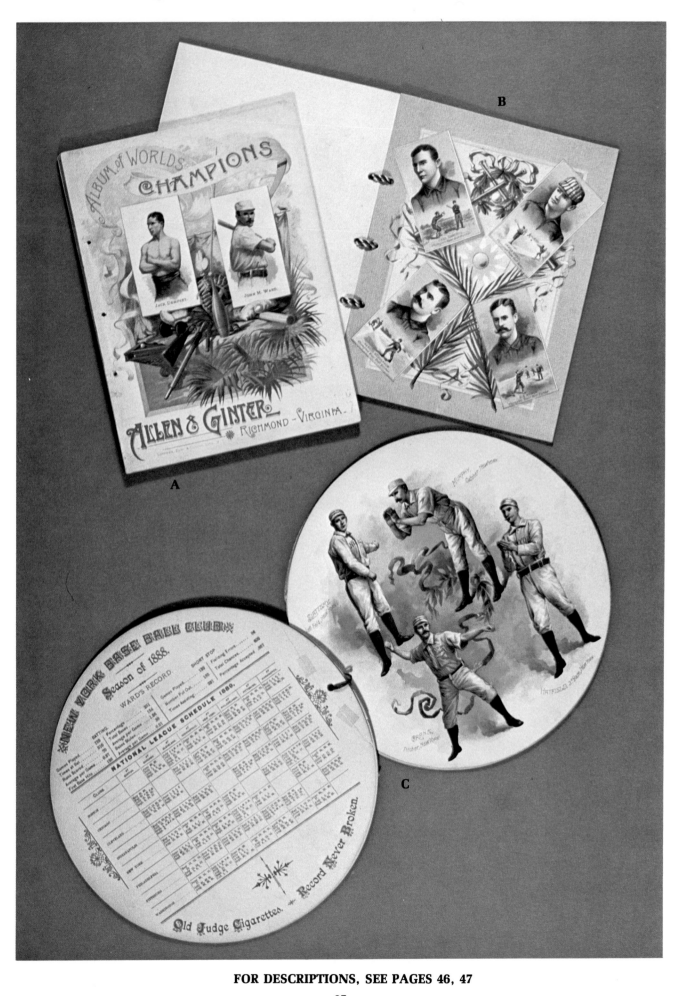

A

B

C

FOR DESCRIPTIONS, SEE PAGES 46, 47

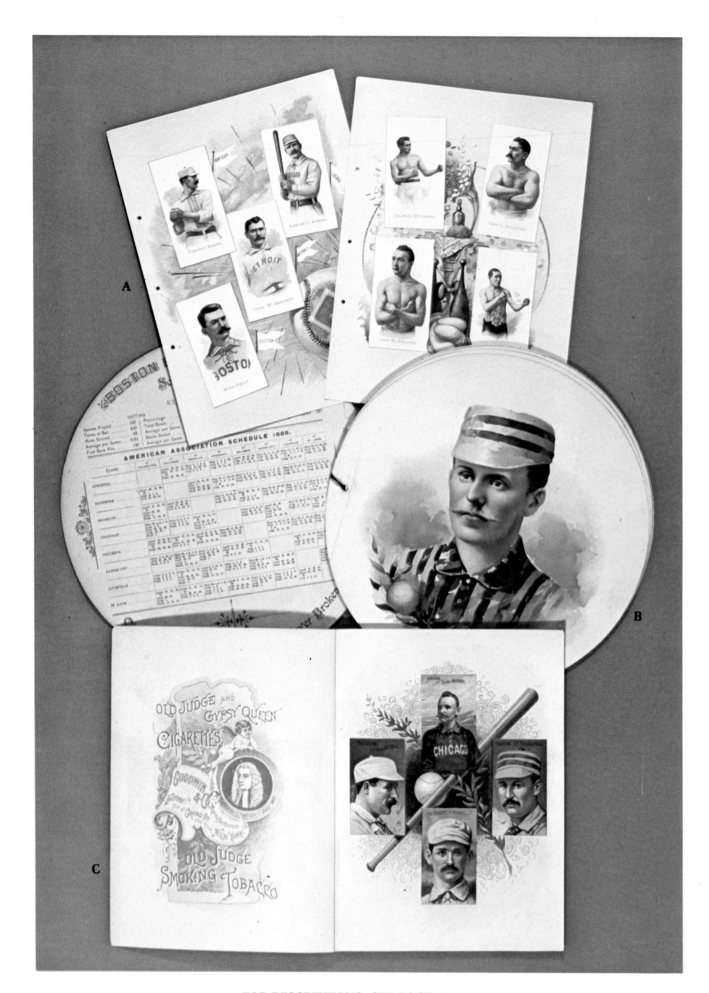

A

B

C

FOR DESCRIPTIONS, SEE PAGE 47

FOR DESCRIPTIONS, SEE PAGES 47, 48

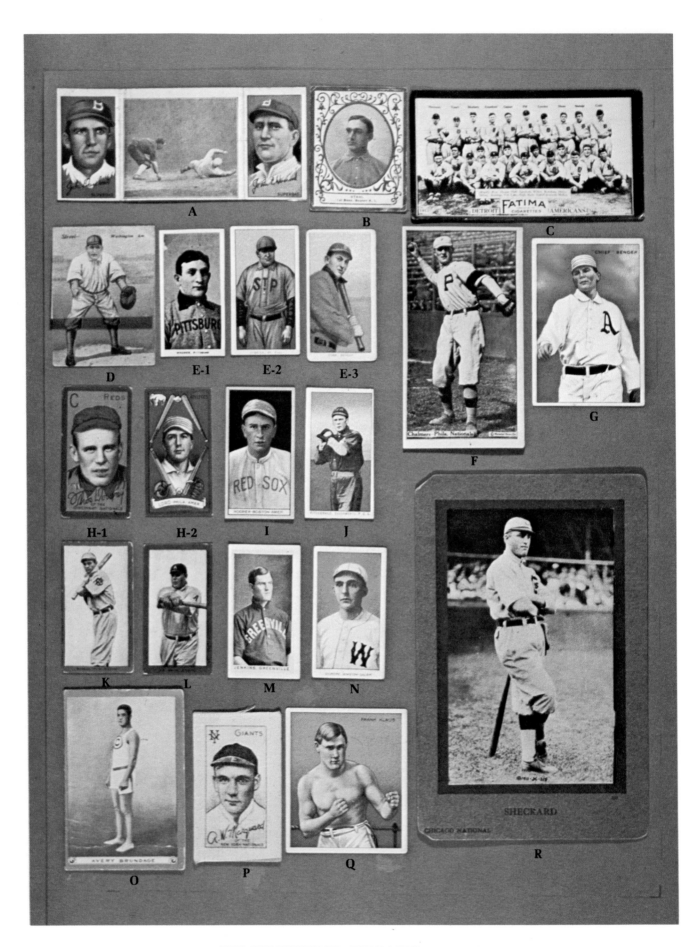

FOR DESCRIPTIONS, SEE PAGES 48, 49, 50

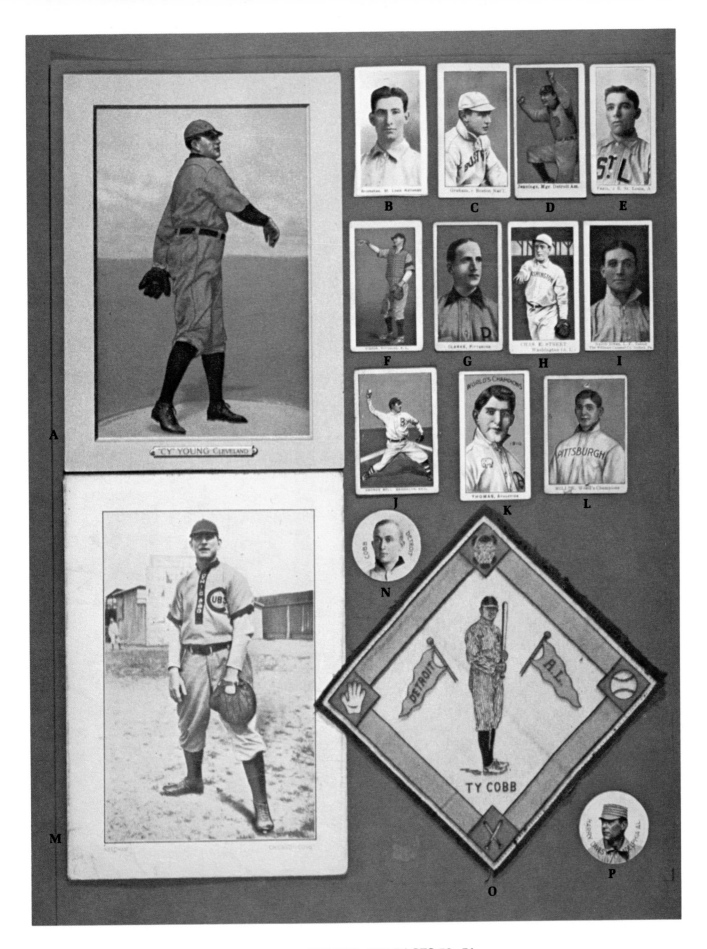

FOR DESCRIPTIONS, SEE PAGES 50, 51

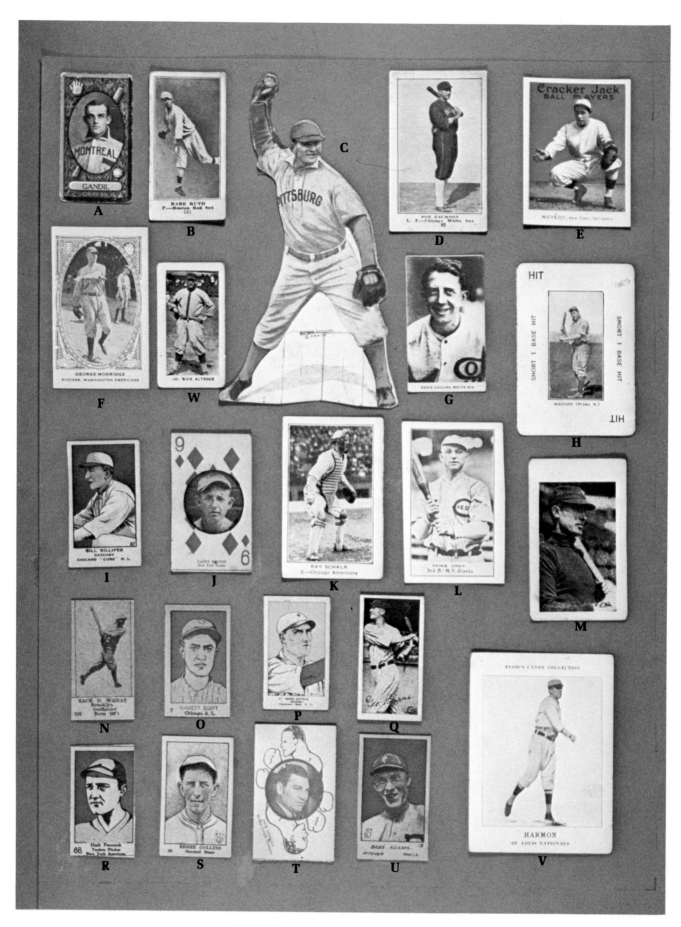

FOR DESCRIPTIONS, SEE PAGES 51, 52

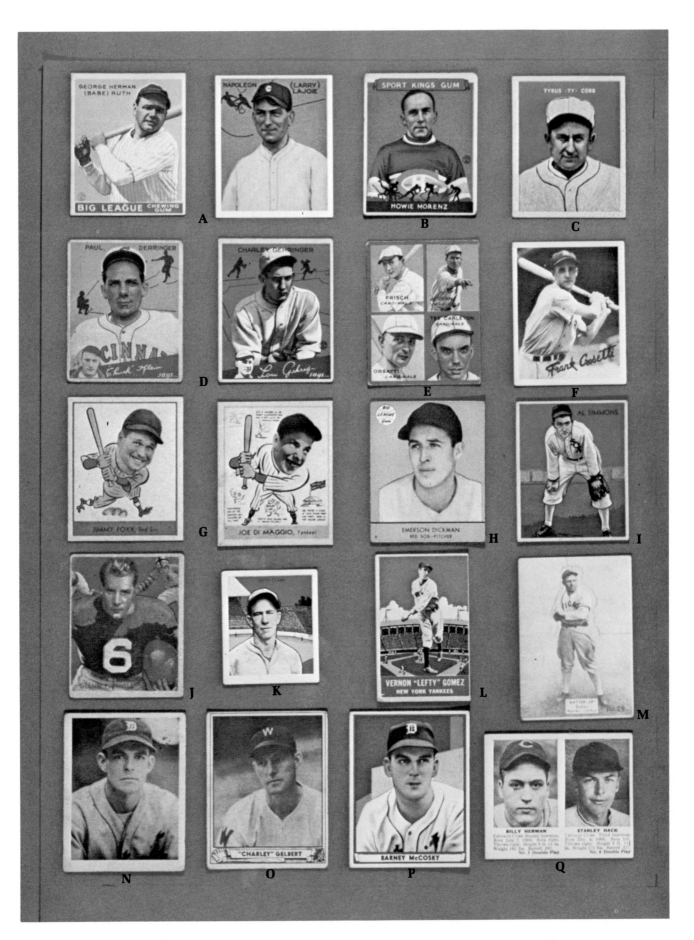

FOR DESCRIPTIONS, SEE PAGES 53, 54

A

B

C

D

E

F

G

H

I-1

I-2

I-3

I-4

FOR DESCRIPTIONS, SEE PAGE 54

A MARTIN MARION

B SPORT THRILLS / WINNING RUN

C

D BOBBIE "BLONDE BOMBER" LAYNE

E

F TONY ZALE

G

H-1 EMIL "DUTCH" LEONARD

H-2

I

J

K ROYAL STARS OF BASEBALL No. 5 / WARREN SPAHN

L JOE GARAGIOLA

M BALL

N

O KEN CARPENTER

P BOB CAREY

Q BOB WELLMAN

R

S PEE WEE REESE / SHORTSTOP BROOKLYN DODGERS / 1952 RED MAN ALL-STAR TEAM / NATIONAL LEAGUE SERIES—PLAYER #17

T

U-1 CHUCK BEDNARIK

U-2 CHUCK ORTMANN

V

W

X Wayne TERWILLIGER / WASHINGTON SENATORS

Y JERSEY JOE WALCOTT

Z TONY CURCILLO / CARDINALS

AA

FOR DESCRIPTIONS, SEE PAGES 55, 56

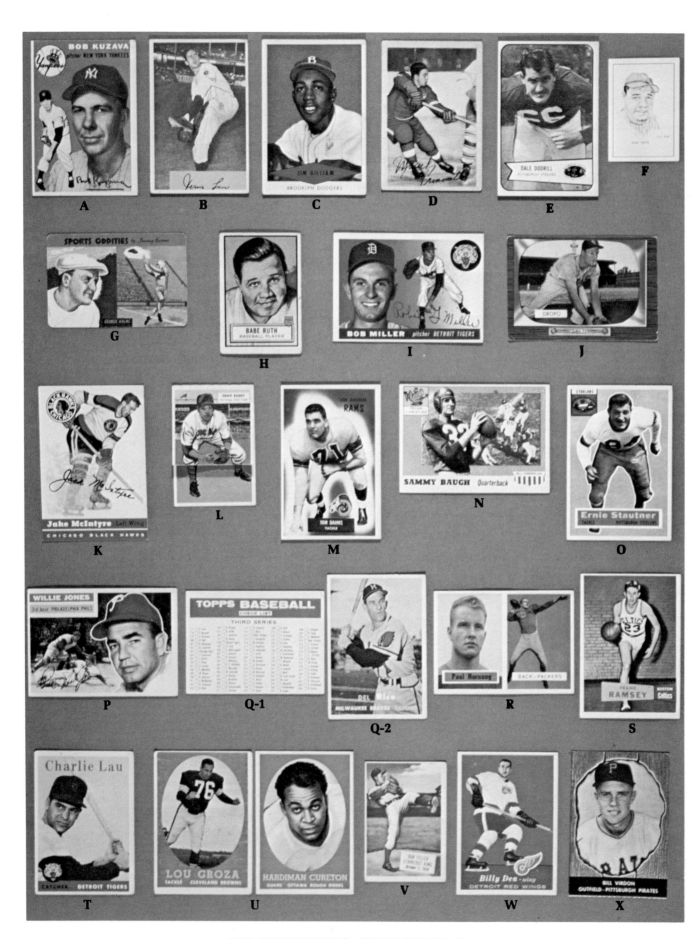

A B C D E F

G H I J

K L M N O

P Q-1 Q-2 R S

T U V W X

FOR DESCRIPTIONS, SEE PAGES 56, 57

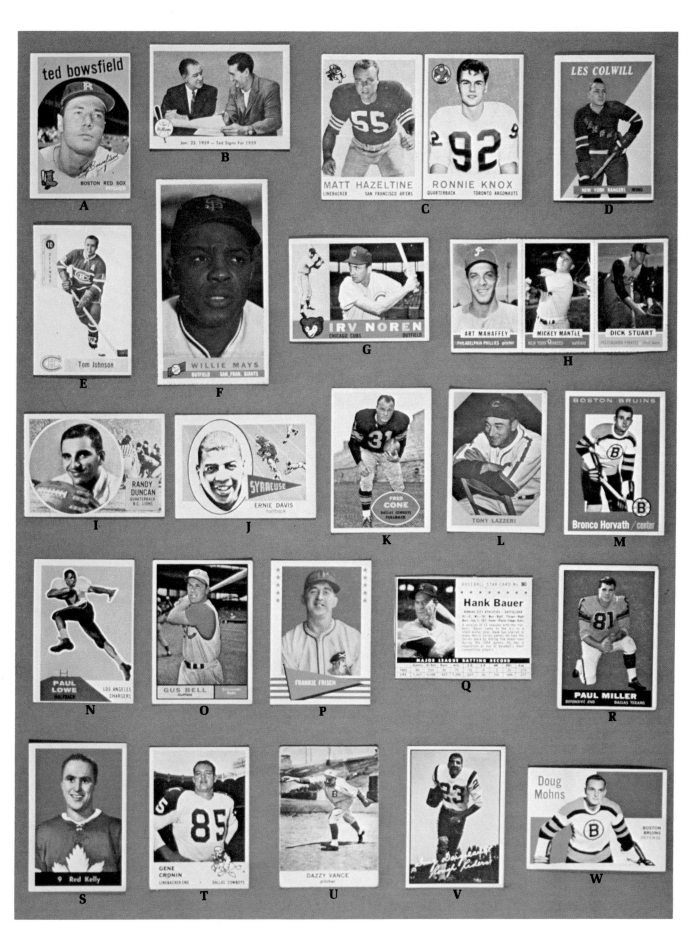

FOR DESCRIPTIONS, SEE PAGES 58, 59

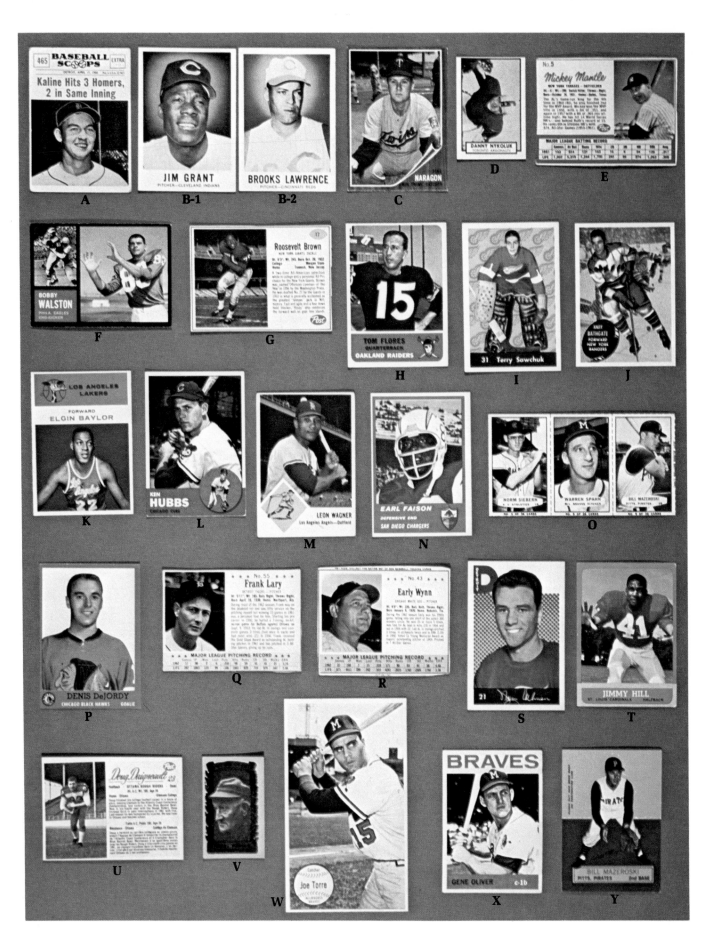

FOR DESCRIPTIONS, SEE PAGES 59, 60

A

B GINO CAPPALLETTI

C Bobby HULL CHICAGO BLACK HAWKS

D BILL BROWN

E RED WINGS ROGER CROZIER goalie

F CHUCK ESTRADA

G PAUL HORNUNG

H BOSTON BABE PARILLI quarterback

I BILLY WILLIAMS

J VERLON BIGGS

K JIM RINGO

L PETE ROSE 2nd base

M-1 ALL-TIME GREATS WALTER JOHNSON WASHINGTON SENATORS Pitcher

M-2 BASEBALL EXTRA — HR ALMOST HIT OUT OF STADIUM — Foxx Socks Into Upper Stands

N TED UHLAENDER · OF TWINS

O BILLY WILLIAMS CUBS

P JIM TYRER TACKLE

Q DOUBLE RUNNERS ADVANCE 2 BASES

R Tony Horton—1B Cleveland Indians

S BART STARR

T DAVE WHITSELL

U JEAN RATELLE

V "HONUS" WAGNER

W SANDERSON

X TIM McCARVER Catcher CARDS

FOR DESCRIPTIONS, SEE PAGES 60, 61

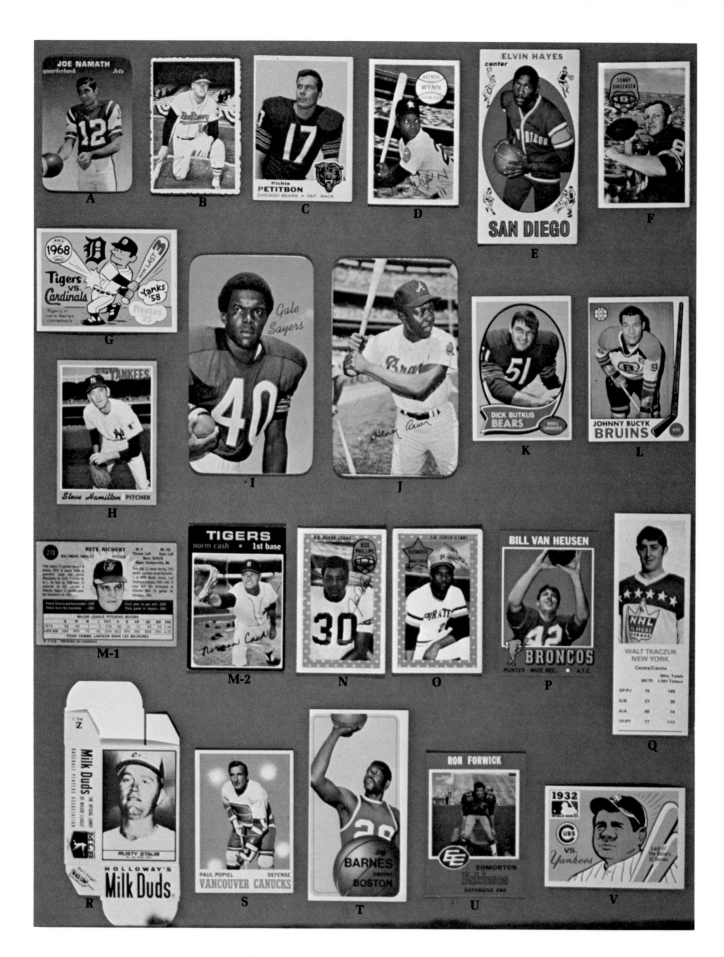

FOR DESCRIPTIONS, SEE PAGES 61, 62

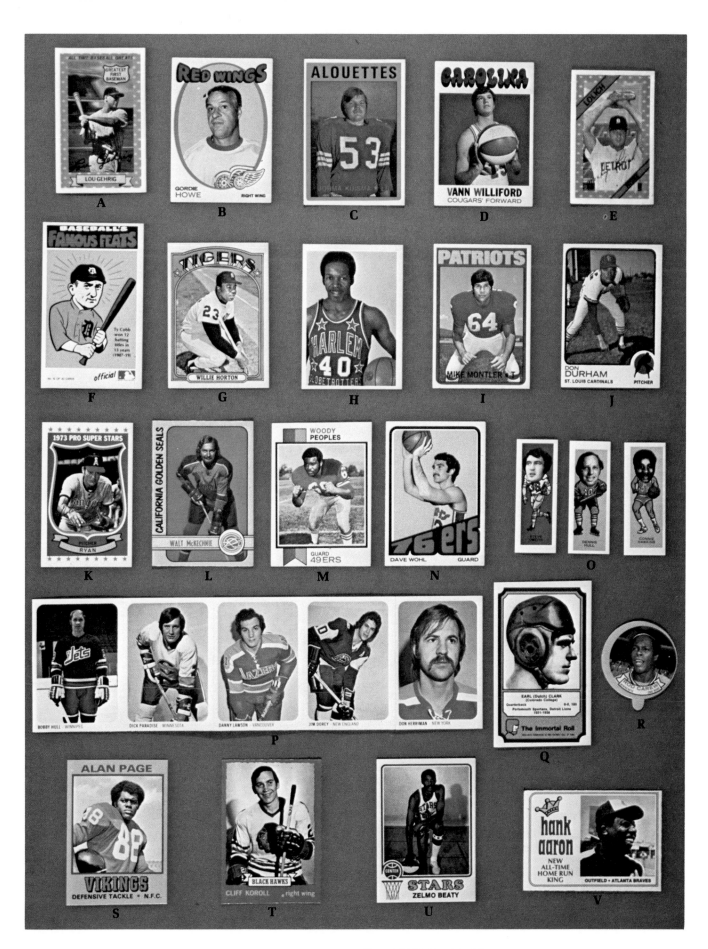

A B C D E
F G H I J
K L M N O
P Q R
S T U V

FOR DESCRIPTIONS, SEE PAGES 62, 63, 64

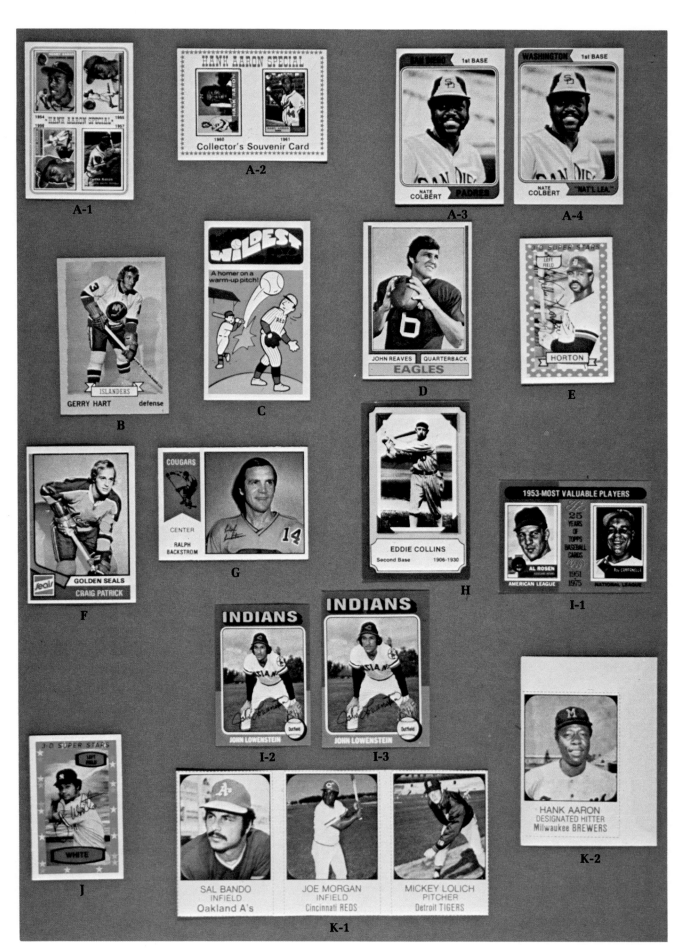

A-1

A-2
Collector's Souvenir Card

A-3
NATE COLBERT · PADRES

A-4
NATE COLBERT · "NAT'L LEA."

B
GERRY HART   defense

C

D
JOHN REAVES   QUARTERBACK
EAGLES

E
HORTON

F
GOLDEN SEALS
CRAIG PATRICK

G
COUGARS
CENTER
RALPH BACKSTROM

H
EDDIE COLLINS
Second Base   1906-1930

I-1
1953-MOST VALUABLE PLAYERS
AL ROSEN · AMERICAN LEAGUE   ROY CAMPANELLA · NATIONAL LEAGUE

I-2
INDIANS
JOHN LOWENSTEIN

I-3
INDIANS
JOHN LOWENSTEIN

J
WHITE

K-1
SAL BANDO · INFIELD · Oakland A's   JOE MORGAN · INFIELD · Cincinnati REDS   MICKEY LOLICH · PITCHER · Detroit TIGERS

K-2
HANK AARON
DESIGNATED HITTER
Milwaukee BREWERS

FOR DESCRIPTIONS, SEE PAGE 64

1975 TOPPS BASKETBALL: this set is complete at 264 cards. The backs feature one of the most attractive layouts and color combinations found in any issue.

1976 TOPPS HOCKEY: this American set is complete with 330 different cards. As hockey has become more acceptable to the American youth, the sets have increased in size. Topps' first hockey set 20 years earlier included only 60 cards.

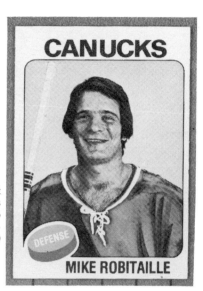

1976 TOPPS BASEBALL: this set is composed of 660 regular numbers, and a 44-card 'traded' set. The picture quality of this set is a marked improvement over the Topps' releases of the previous five years.

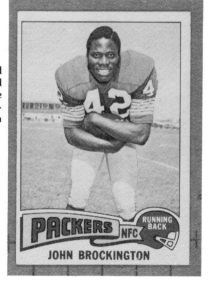

1976 KELLOG'S 3-D BASEBALL: there are 57 cards in the complete set. Like most of the other issues released by Kellogg's, the set was available by responding to an offer found on the product's box.

1975 TOPPS FOOTBALL: the 528-card set-size of 1973 and '74 was continued for this edition. One can trace the growth of professional football by comparing the sizes of the card sets from year to year.

Regional Trading Cards

In general, the sports trading cards that have the highest value are those that were issued on a regional basis. Unlike the cards issued with gum, or with cereal, these cards came with such products as hot dogs, bread, milk, gasoline, newspapers, potato chips, banks, soft drinks and cookies. The cards usually feature players that perform for teams in the city, or area, in which they are being distributed. There was often little fanfare assigned to their promotion, press runs were considerably smaller than those of the national issues, and many were not even popular with the audience to which they were being directed — the youngsters.

The single most important factor in the escalated values of these cards is supply and demand. The demand is high; the supply is sometimes almost non-existent. Some regional cards demand prices of as much as $100 a card. This has led a number of collectors to place ads in newspapers in the areas in which the cards were distributed in hopes of finding their missing numbers.

On the following pages over 75 samples of regional cards have been assembled. Included in this group you will find some of the most valuable, some of the rarest, some of the plainest, and some of the most common.

1915 Fleischmann/Ferguson Bakery—issued by two bakeries as an insert in their products. Cards are unnumbered, and exact number in a complete set is not known. Cards contained a tab at bottom that was redeemable for an album to display the pictures. Statement on tab reads, "Will hold 100 photos," which leads many to believe that at least 100 were issued.

1928 Yuengling's Ice Cream—this issue includes 60 numbered, black and white photos. The player's name and card number appear on the card fronts. The cards were redeemed for ice cream products.

1937 Dixie Cup Lids—this set is complete at 10. Circular cardboard with player head shots. Includes 7 baseball personalities (two different poses of Carl Hubbell) and 3 from other sports. There are many different varieties of the color of the half-tones. Came with ice cream products. Similar set was issued in 1938.

1912 Home Run Kisses—some collectors would argue with inserting this set into a regional category instead of with the early candy issues. They were issued by the Collins-McCarthy Candy Co. There distribution was confined to the San Francisco area. There are 90 known cards in this unnumbered set.

1947 Signal Oil Baseball—this set features sketches of members of Pacific Coast League players. There are 89 pictures in the unnumbered set.

1947 Tip Top Bread—this set was issued in eleven different areas of the country. Only cards of the local team were available in any of the areas. The cards are black and white, and are unnumbered. There are 165 known cards. The card pictured is that of John Berardino, now the star of the soap opera "General Hospital."

1949 Sealtest Phillies—this set is very similar to the Lummis Peanut Butter issue of the same year. The 'card' is actually a small bumper sticker with removable paper coating that protects a self-adhesive back. It is believed that this set contains the same 7 players as in the Lummis set.

1949 Remar Bread—the Remar Company issued sets of cards picturing members of the Oakland Oaks baseball team from 1946-1950. The cards are black and white, and this particular issue is unnumbered.

1950 Drake's Cookies—there are 36 different players highlighted in this set. The cards include dark blue borders, and are numbered. Most of those pictures are from New York teams. The card shown is that of Carl Furillo.

1953 Glendale Meats—27 players of the Detroit Tigers are pictured. This is one of the most popular regional sets ever issued. The cards, unlike many other meat product cards, was not part of the package stiffener. The cards are unnumbered. The card of Art Houttemann is almost non-existent: one of the rarest of all sports cards.

1952 Num Num Potato Chips—there are 20, numbered black and white pictures in this set. The card bottoms contain a coupon that was clipped off to receive a free autographed baseball. Card #16, Bob Kennedy, is particularly hard to find.

1952 Mother's Cookies—there are 64 Coast League players in this colorful set. Several variations exist, making the total number of different cards 72. The pictured's name is printed on the card fronts. The cards are numbered.

1951 Hage's Ice Cream—set consists of 38 cards. Several players are pictured on more than one card. Cards are not numbered, and include players on the San Diego Padres minor league team, and 6 from the parent Cleveland Indian squad. Hage's issued similar sets in 1949, 1950 and '52.

1953 Hunter's Wieners—featured are 26 players of the St. Louis Cardinals. Cards are unnumbered, blank-backed, full-color fronts. Similar sets were issued by Hunter in 1954 and '55.

1953 Mother's Cookies—this set features 63 players from the Pacific Coast League. The player's facsimile autograph appears on the card fronts. The cards are numbered.

1953 Johnston's Cookies—cards are numbered 1-25 and feature players on the Milwaukee Braves. Card backs include full biographical information on the subjects.

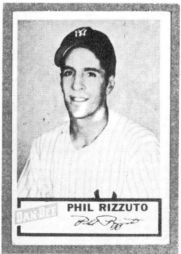

1953 Dan Dee Potato Chips—this set is complete at 29. The cards were heavily waxed and found in packages of potato chips. They are not numbered. The cards of Walker Cooper and Paul Smith, both Pirates, are scarce. The Mickey Mantle card also commands a premium price.

1954 Stahl-Meyer Franks—this set of 12 reported cards features players from the three New York teams. The fronts are in full color, the backs include statistical information. The cards are unnumbered. The cards are waxed, as they were the package stiffeners. The company issued similar sets in 1953 and 1955.

1954 Johnston's Cookies—this is the smallest size of the three Johnston issues. The card numbers correspond to the player's uniform number. There are 35 Milwaukee Brave personalities featured.

1954 Baltimore Weiners Baseball—this set of 36 cards was manufactured by the Esskay Meat Co., and highlights players on the first Oriole team in Baltimore. The card fronts are in full color and are not numbered.

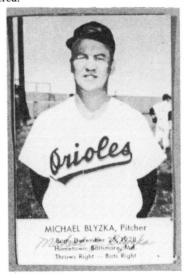

1954 Wilson Wieners Baseball—this set is complete at 20 cards. One of the most popular regional sets ever issued because of its large geographic distribution. Cards are unnumbered, full color fronts.

1954 N.Y. Journal-American Baseball—this set of cards was actually used as a lottery-type contest by the sponsoring newspaper. The set features 19 Dodgers, and 20 players from both Yanks and Giants. A 20th Dodger may have been issued. Cards contained a lucky number Winners were announced daily.

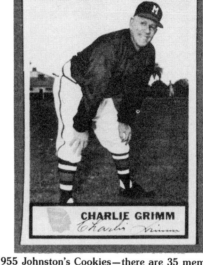

1955 Old Homestead Bruins—there are 21 known cards in this set of cards featuring members of the Des Moines Bruins minor league team. The cards are black and white and carry no biographical information, however, there are many major league players in the set. The cards are also not numbered.

1955 Johnston's Cookies—there are 35 members of the Brave organization spotlighted in this set. The cards were found in the packages in strips of six. The side edges of the cards have perforations where they were designed to be torn into single cards. Card numbers match uniform numbers.

1955 Rodeo Meats Baseball—there are 38 different players in this set which features players of the Kansas City Athletics. Eight of the players' cards exist with two different colored backgrounds, making the total of 46 known cards. An album which was abailable through the sponsoring company indicates that cards of Burleigh Grimes and Dick Kryhoski are in the set, although neither has been reported by collectors who have these cards. The cards are not numbered. Twelve of the players in the '55 set were reissued in 1956. The information on ordering the album is not included on the cards issued in 1956.

1958 Bond Bread—there are 9 different players, all from the Buffalo Bisons of the International League. The cards are not numbered.

1956 Spic & Span Dry Cleaners—some collectors regard this issue as a postcard, others as a regional card issue. There are 17 known players in the set. The fronts are black and white, and are not numbered. the players featured, most members of the great Milwaukee teams of 1957 and 1958, make this a very popular set with Braves fans.

1957 Swift Major League Baseball Stars—this unique set of 18 cards was found in the packages of franks. The cards are die cut to allow the pieces to easily come out of the form. The 7-8 pieces on each card can be assembled to form a 3-D statue of the player. Very scarce because most youngsters assembled the figures.

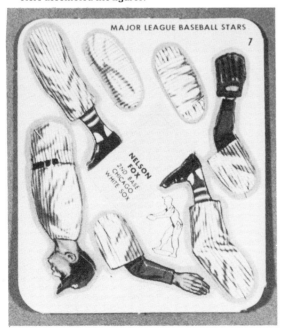

1958 Bell Brand Dodgers—set of 10 cards was included in corn chip product packages. Cards are unnumbered, green bordered with mahogany half-tone pictures. Cards of Duke Snider and Gino Cimoli are scarce.

1959 Prize Franks—only known card is this one of Wertz.

1960 Armour Denver Bears—set features players on Denver's minor league entry. Exact number in this set is unknown. There are 10 cards reported, to date. Set was issued with meat products. The cards are not numbered.

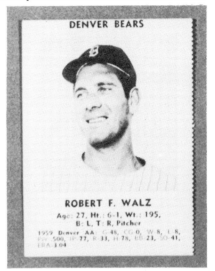

1960 Lake to Lake Braves—issued by dairy company in the Milwaukee area. The cards are blue and white and apparently were torn from a coupon book by milk truck drivers. The cards were redeemable for several novelty items. The card of Billy Bruton is scarce. The cards are not numbered; there are 28.

1960 Morrell meats Baseball—the set is complete at 12 cards. Cards are unnumbered, and in full color. Card backs contain full biographical information.

1960 Darigold Farms—there are 14 known cards in this set of Spokane Indian players. The cards are numbered, and many collectors feel that the set actually contains 24 cards.

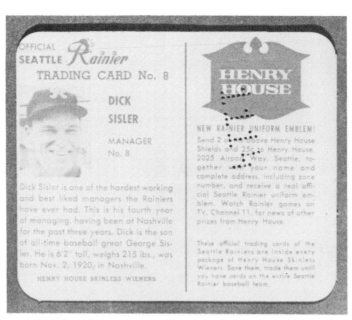

1960 Henry House Wieners Baseball—this set highlights 18 players on the Seattle Ranier club. The players' uniform number is the card number. The cards, so typical of hot dog issues, are the supportive part of the packaging.

1960 Tacoma Bank—there are 21 unnumbered cards in this set. The card fronts are in color and picture members of Tacoma's PCL entry.

1961 Tacoma Bank—the set features members of the Tacoma Giants PCL team. There are 21, unnumbered, sepia colored cards in a complete set.

JIM RINGO
No. 51 C Ht. 6-1 Wt. 235 Syracuse

1961 Lake to Lake Packers—there are 36 numbered cards in this set distributed in the Wisconsin area. The cards are green and white. They were distributed with home deliveries of dairy products, and they could be redeemed for several different Packer novelty items.

1961 Cloverleaf Dairy Twins—there are 16 known cards in this set. The cards are green, black and white and include player statistics from the 1960 season. The cards were located on a side panel of half gallons of milk. A similar set was issued the following year.

BILL TUTTLE, outfielder

Home: Raytown, Missouri. Age 31. Height 6 ft. Weight 185 lbs. Bats and throws right-handed.

1961 Union Oil—there are 67 known players in this set which features players from six Pacific Coast teams. The cards of the local team were available only in that area. All of the cards are unnumbered, with the exception of the Tacoma team.

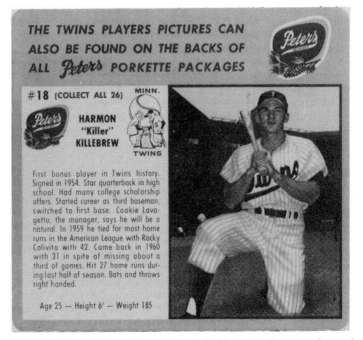

1961 Peters Meats Twins—26 members of the Minnesota Twins are featured. This set was issued the first year after the Senators' move to the Twin Cities. The card backgrounds are yellow, and the pictures in full color. Unlike so many other regional sets, there are no scarce cards.

1963 Milwaukee Sausage Baseball—this set of 11 cards was issued by the Milwaukee Sausage Co. of Seattle. It features players from the Rainiers minor league team. The cards are unnumbered, and were the stiffener in the packages.

Babe Ruth Playing Card—issued in the 1960's, this is the back side of a deck of playing cards. Several such sports scenes are now sought by baseball card collectors.

Compliments of Kahn's
"THE WIENER THE WORLD AWAITED"

1962 Kahn's Baseball—the Kahn Meat Company issued trading cards with their products from 1955 through 1969. For two reasons, this is probably the most popular of all regional issues. First, the relatively wide distribution of the products made the cards' supply plentiful enough to capture the interest of a large number of collectors; and secondly, the cards were printed for 15 years. The tradition that was established by prior issues continued each year. The card pictured is from the 1962 set. The sets issued from 1955-63 are black and white.

Wilson Sporting Goods Baseball—issued in the early 60's, there are three known players in this set. The narrow cards are believed to be a side panel from boxes containing Wilson ball gloves. There are questions among collectors regarding this issue. Some feel that it is not a legitimate 'card' issue, while others feel it should be catalogued with the Topps' issues as a nation-wide issue.

1961 Bell Brand Dogers—this set features 20 members of the Los Angeles Dodgers team. The cards are numbered by uniform numbers and contain statistical records through the 1960 season. The set was distributed with potato chip products.

WALLY MOON
OUTFIELDER   L.A. DODGERS

1963 Marhoefer Indy 500 Winners—this unique set features winners of racing's most famous race. The pictures are black and white, and are heavily waxed, as they were the package stiffeners. The card pictured is that of Roger Ward, two-time winner of the classic.

1970 Washington Traffic Safety Baseball—this set is complete at 10 cards. The cards are unnumbered, and are blank on the reverse side.

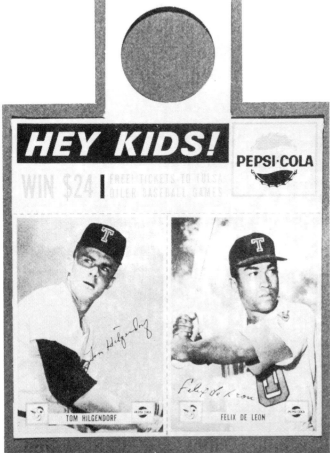

1963 Pepsi Tulsa Oilers—this set of 24 cards was obtained by purchasing soft drink cases that contained twelve different cards/advertising notices. Similar sets were issued in 1962 and 1966. The cards are not numbered.

93

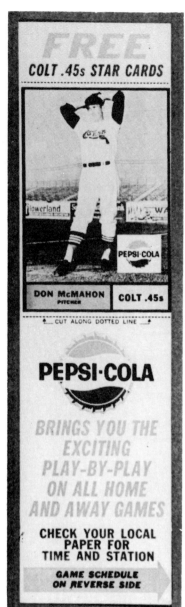

1964 Meadowgold Dairy—the four pictures shown are the complete set. The four were found on one side panel from a half gallon of milk.

1963 Pepsi Colt .45's—this set is comprised of 16 cards. The cards were found in soft drink packages, one card to a strip. The cards are unnumbered, and the photos are black and white. The cards of Warwick and Bateman were used as test items, and are considered scarce.

1967 Philadelphia Safe Driving Baseball—there are 13 cards in this set. The cards are numbered by the player's uniform number, and are blank-backed.

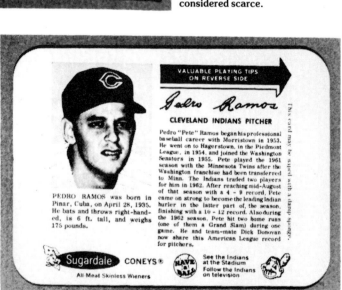

1963 Sugardale Franks—there are 31 known cards in this black and white set. The cards were part of the frankfurter package. The set features players from the Cleveland and Pittsburgh clubs.

94

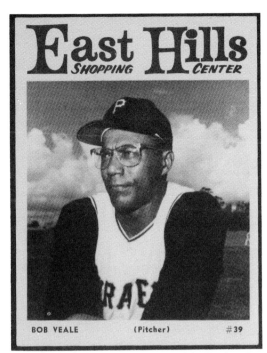

BOB VEALE   (Pitcher)   #39

1966 East Hills Pirates—this set of 25 Pittsburgh Pirates was distributed by the East Hills Shopping Center. The cards were distributed in sets, so there are no rare or scarce numbers. The cards are numbered with the player's uniform number. The photos are in full-color and are blank backed.

1967 Irvingdale Dairy Braves—set of four cards were included on the panel of milk cartons. Backs are blank, cards not numbered. In addition to the two cards pictured, Mack Jones and Denis Menke comprise the remainder of the set.

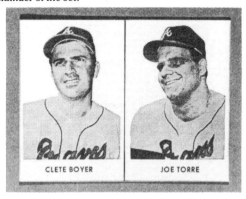

CLETE BOYER   JOE TORRE

1964 Kahn's Baseball—issued with hot dogs. Set consists of 31 players from the Reds, Indians and Pirates. Cards are in full color, and contain facsimile player autographs. The card shown is Tommy Harper of Cincinnati. The 1965 set is very similar, but also contains players from Milwaukee.

1966 Kahn's Baseball—this set is complete at 32 cards. Cards are found with, and without, the Kahn's advertisement. The cards are in full color, with facsimile autographs.

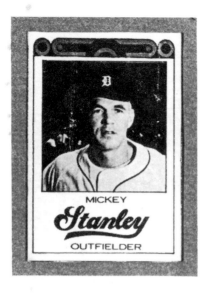

1968 Free Press Bubblegumless Cards—there are 28 'cards' in this unusual set. The pictures were a part of Sunday magazine supplements of the **Detroit Free Press**. Many collectors clipped out the fronts, and backs, and pasted them on cardboard to make a 'card.' The pictures are in color, and are not numbered.

Sunny Ayr Farms Dairy—issued probably during the 1968 season. The card of Callison is the only know player.

Cards from Japan—pictured are two cards from the many sets that have been issued in the last ten years featuring players in Japanese baseball. These cards are becoming more popular with collectors for two reasons: first, an ever increasing number of American ballplayers are going to Japan to play ball, making their cards recognizable as well as in demand; secondly, it offers still another area for the collector to concentrate his efforts. The card on the left is that of Japanese home run champion Sadaharu Oh.

1971 Jack in the Box Angels—this set is complete at 10 cards. The photos are black and white, printed on a buff colored paper stock. The backs are blank, and the cards are not numbered.

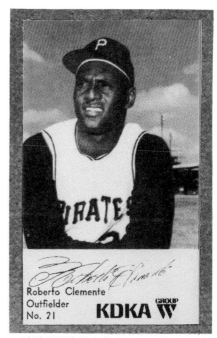

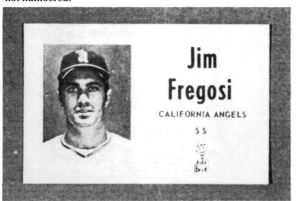

1968 KDKA/Arby's Pirates—this set of 23 full color cards was distributed at Arby's restaurants, but carries promotional information for KDKA Radio-TV, the Pirates flagship station. The cards are numbered by the player's uniform number.

1970 McDonald's Milwaukee Brewers—set is complete at 31 cards. Backs are blank, sketches on card fronts are in full color.

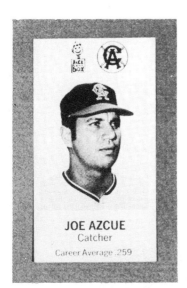

1969 Jack in the Box Angels—this set of 13 California Angels players was distributed by a hamburger chain in the southern California area. The cards are black and white, blank-backed, and unnumbered.

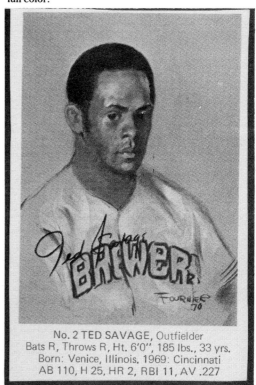

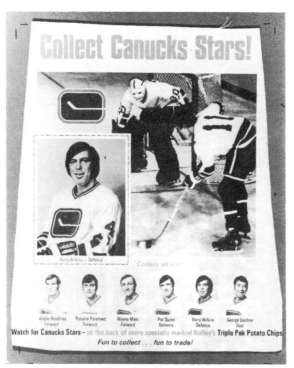

1973 Nalley's Potato Chips—this set features 6 members of the Vancouver Canuck hockey team. The cards were found on the backs of cardboard potato chip boxes. (All 6 available cards are pictured on the bottom of this panel).

1972 McDonald's Floridians—this set of 10 cards was redeemable for a free basketball. The card bottoms contained a stub that was used for free admission to Floridian games by youngsters. The cards are in full color, and are not numbered.

1972 Bowery Bank DiMaggio—this single card was issued as part of an advertising campaign by the Bowery Bank of New York City in 1972. Dealers bought up the remaining stock making this regional card a 'national' issue.

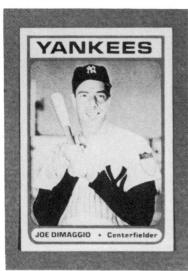

1972 Icee Bear Basketball—there are 19 known cards in this set which was distributed in many Woolworth stores with the purchase of slurpee products. The cards are in full color, and are not numbered.

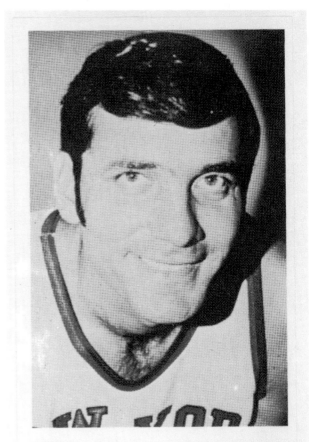

JERRY LUCAS
NEW YORK
FORWARD

1973 Putney Road Market—this set is complete at one card. The Road Market issued this picture of local hero Carlton Fisk which includes a summary of his career highlights on the back. The Brattleboro, Vermont establishment also named a cut of meat in honor of the Boston catcher. (This card has been personally autographed "Pudge Fisk.")

BOB UECKER
RADIO, PLAY-BY-PLAY
MILWAUKEE BREWERS

1975 Brewers Broadcasting—this unique set of 7 cards features the two radio and two television broadcasters for the Brewers. These first four cards are numbered. The remaining three cards list the schedule of broadcasts, and are not numbered. The cards are blue, orange and white. The set was distributed by KTMJ, the Brewers' flagship network station.

WICHITA AEROS

PETE LACOCK
Outfielder

Card 124

1974 Wichita Aeros Baseball—set of 28 different players from the Wichita AAA team are spotlighted. The sets were produced by One Day Film Service of Wichita, Kansas. The cards are black and white and numbered 101-128. The card of Badcock has a variety spelled 'Babcock,' and the card of Hiser also exists without his picture; this being the rare version.

Musketeers

MIKE NOEL

1974-75 Sioux City Muskateers Hockey—set consists of 20 players. Green half-tones on yellow stock, unnumbered. Player's uniform number on card backs.

1974 Padre Foto-Ball Cards—this unique set of 15 circular cards was issued in conjunction with the McDonald's restaurants in the San Diego area. Fans attending a special night at the San Diego Stadium were given five cards, and a plastic baseball storage container. The remaining cards were given away on other specially designated dates. The complete set, with the ball, were also available as a package unit following the season.

1976 Baseball Player Discs—set includes 70 different players. The discs were issued in six parts of the country. Six different card sponsor's logos appear on the card backs.

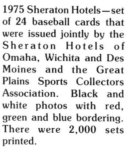

1975 Shakey's Pizza—this 18 card set was issued in conjunction with the West Coast Sports Collectors Association. The first card, Joe DiMaggio, was given to persons attending the collectors convention. It was used for discount purchases at the Shakey's restaurants. The cards are numbered on the fronts.

1975 Sheraton Hotels—set of 24 baseball cards that were issued jointly by the Sheraton Hotels of Omaha, Wichita and Des Moines and the Great Plains Sports Collectors Association. Black and white photos with red, green and blue bordering. There were 2,000 sets printed.

Premiums

Premiums are those items that were available to the public by redeeming coupons, wrappers, boxes, cards, etc. These items were usually advertised on the back of a trading card, or on the product's wrapper. Others were publicized through signs or posters at the establishment selling the original products. Some of these were ordered through mail order addresses, others could be picked up at the neighborhood merchant's store. Most required no additional expenditure on the part of the customer.

Business firms have offered premium items for years. The first sports premiums were the large baseball pictures presented to smokers before the turn of the century by the various tobacco companies. Other items offered have included felt pennants, baseball games, magic rings, pins, booklets, posters, albums, and uncut sheets of trading cards; to name a few.

The most popular premium items have been the baseball pictures. Most collectors of trading cards are also very interested in these issues. Some of these premium issues have such a close resemblance to trading card editions that they have been included in that section.

The value of premiums, like most everything else, is dictated by supply and demand. Those in demand, primarily the large baseball pictures, have an accompaning low supply. Items produced for premium distribution usually had a very short production run. As easy as it was for youngsters to redeem gum wrappers for the bigger photos of their favorite players; a relatively very small group participated.

Included in this section are illustrations of some of the more universal items that were offered on a premium basis. Other premiums that appear in the trading card section are so indicated in their descriptive summaries.

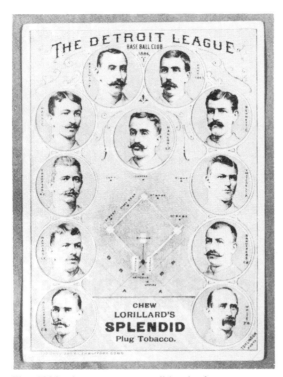

This 1886 release may very well be the first sports premium. It was distributed by the Lorillard Tobacco Company, probably through its dealers. Pictured are eleven members of the 1886 Detroit team that played in the National League.

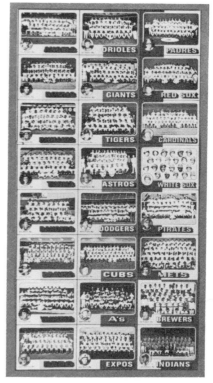

This set of 24 uncut 1975 team cards was available by sending wrappers and 25¢ to the Topps Company. A similar offer existed in 1974.

This black and white premium was distributed by the Goudey Gum Company in 1939. The backs of these photos include instructional pointers on various aspects of the game of baseball. There were **24** different performers pictured in the set, issued in 1939.

This attractive cabinet photo was available from the publishers of **Sporting Life** in 1909. **Sporting Life** was a popular sports-oriented publication. Subscribers could choose from over 350 subjects listed. The photo sold for 10¢, or twelve for $1.00.

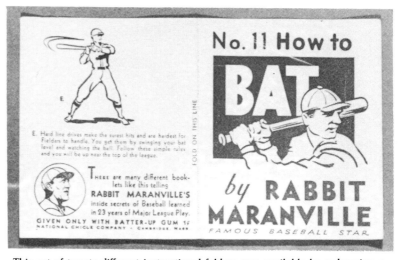

This set of twenty different instructional folders was available by redeeming a number of National Chicle wrappers with the local dealer. All of these folders feature tips from Rabbit Maranville. Their release date is believed to have been 1935 or '36.

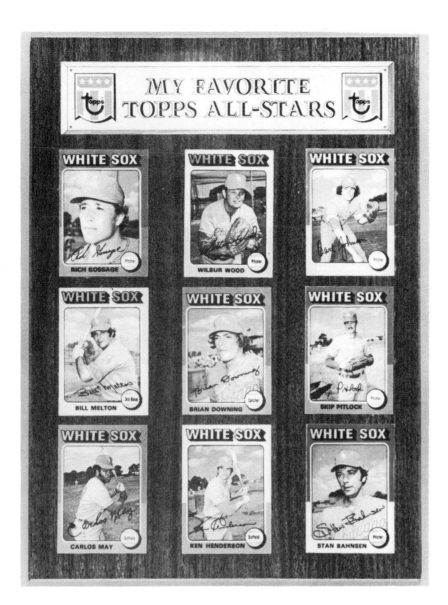

One of the most unique offers made by a company was this laminated plaque that was available from Topps for a wrapper and $4.25. The collector also sent to the Company the nine cards he wished to be mounted.

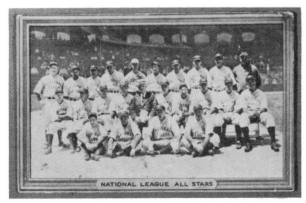

This 1934 premium was available from the Goudey Gum Company in exchange for ten wrappers from their 1¢ packages of bubble gum. Other popular selections from this set of seven were Babe Ruth and Lou Gehrig.

This spiral-bound booklet was available by writing to the address printed on the wrappers of the 1975 Milwaukee Brewers Broadcasters cards printed by WTMJ Radio-Television in Milwaukee.

Goudey also issued a set that was slightly smaller in size in 1939. There were 48 different players featured. This lesser-sized series is referred to as type 'A', the larger edition, 'B.'

This picture of Babe Ruth was one of several that were availble from the Leaf Gum Company. Others included Alexander, Mathewson, McGraw, Walsh, Johnson, Cochrane and Gehrig. The premiums were released in 1949.

One of the few full-color picture premiums, this set of fifty different photos was available through the National Chicle Company in 1935. Several selections included multiple player poses and action shots.

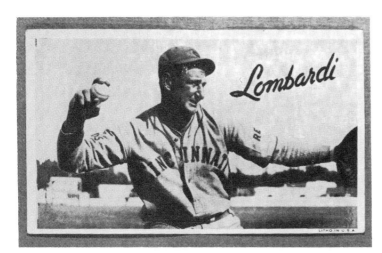

The mostly commonly seen premium pictures from the thirties are these blank-backed photos. They are commonly called 'Wide Pens,' in contrast to a similar set that used a thinner type for the player's name. This set was distributed by the Goudey Company in 1936. Their plentiful supply is attributed to the fact that these pictures were available from neighborhood merchants rather than from some mail order address.

Errors, Variations and Oddities

Printers have been making mistakes since the press was invented. To the collectors of trading cards, this has represented an on-going challenge. These mistake-plagued cards, and in many cases a second card correcting the inaccuracies of the first, have been the source of nightmares to many a sports hobbyist. For when these blunders are corrected, a scarce card is often created.

The two most common terms used to describe this situation are 'error' and 'variation.' Error cards are those that contain a mistake: statistics that are inaccurate, incorrect pictures, wrong numerical numbering, flaws in ink colors, etc. Error cards are never corrected. If they are, they then become variations. Variations are cards of which at least two different versions exist. One of which usually contains an error of the type described previously. The other(s) are usually corrected versions of the cards that contained the inaccuracies. A third term that is applicable in this area is 'misprint.' Misprints usually occur when the back of one card is printed on the front of another card. This is normally a mechanical, rather than human, miscue.

The value of variation cards is, in most cases, slightly higher than the other cards in any particular set. Many collectors view the whole area of variations as one more obstacle in their quest to complete a set. Some are satisfied in acquiring all of the numbers in an issue rather than every variation. This statement, though, is not universal. Several prominent variations are very much in demand. In the popular White-Bordered tobacco series the card of Sherry Magee of the Philadelphia National League team also exists with his name spelled 'Magie.' This inaccurate version commands a very dear price. The 1960 Sports Novelties' variation of the card of Jim Grant (illustrated on page 76) is another example of a corrected card that is in great demand. Most recently, the series of cards depicting the Padres as "Washington, National League" is also an exception.

New variations and errors are being discovered each year. As more collectors inspect the cards in their collections, the list will continue to grow.

On the following pages a small sampling of these cards is presented. In addition, a few oddities are also pictured. Those wishing to read more about amusing poses and classic blunders that have graced the faces of trading cards are referred to "The Great American Baseball Card Flipping, Trading and Bubble Gum Book."

This card of Henry Aaron would look 'normal' to 99 of 100 persons. The smaller action shot is actually a picture of Willie Mays. His uniform has been retouched to resemble the Milwaukee uniform of 1956. This is an error card.

No doubt the happiest individual pictured in the 1969 Topps baseball set was the California Angels' bat boy. He was mistaken for Aurelio Rodriguez when this picture was taken during spring training.

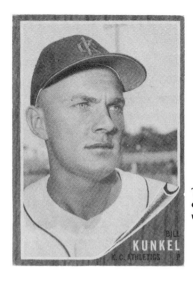

The 1962 Topps baseball set contains eight cards that exist with two photo variations.

This 1958 card contains a picture of Ray Monzant. This is considered an error.

Ron Santo's picture appears on this card of Don Landrum. This is an error.

This picture of Cub third baseman Ken Hubbs was printed as that of Dick Ellsworth. This error card was never corrected.

The picture of Washington pitcher Camilio Pascual was inserted in the circle on this card of Ralph Lumenti. This is an error card.

Colt safetyman Bob Boyd is pictured on this card of Raymond Berry.

This 1916 card of Edd Roush contains a spelling error on the player's last name.

This card of Rookie Stars that appeared in the 1963 Topps set came in two varieties; the correct, and the one indicated as 1962.

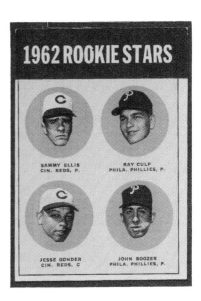

Five team cards in the 1956 Topps set were issued in three different versions. One included the year, 1955, following the name of the team. Another exists without the year, and the name centered in the dark panel. A third version, not pictured, has the team name flush left, with no year designation.

This 1973 Topps test set edition used reprints of the 1953 Topps edition. The painting used for this Carl Furillo card is actually Bill Antonello.

Henry Aaron does not swing the bat from the left side of the plate. An inspection of the uniform numbers shows that the negative was put in the developer backwards. This is considered an error card because the mistake was created during the printing.

This card is considered an error. Not because Burdette is shown as a left-hander, but because his first name is mispelled. Lew 'pulled one' on the Topps photographer by posing with a lefty glove in a wind-up pose.

Postcards

Postcards first appeared in the U.S. in the 1860's. Most of these carried advertisements. Strict postal regulations stunted the evolution of the view cards, popular in Europe, until 1898. By 1904, the postcard was the World's greatest souvenir, and one of the most popular collectables. Few pictures appeared in the newspapers and magazines of that era, and to many people, the postcard was very 'real'. Many collections were started in the period from 1904-14, and can still be found today. The multi-colored postcard began to vanish in the late Teens, and with this practice the popularity in collecting declined. In 1935 the Kodachrome process was developed, and collector interest was rekindled. The general field of postcard collecting is very well developed today. Numerous clubs and organizations exist across the country, and in foreign countries as well. Postcards are not, however, a collectable that has gained universal acceptance among sports hobbyists. Ambiguity associated with the cataloging of postcard-sized (3½ x 5½) cards has been the source of much of this indifference.

The first sports subjects appeared on postcards shortly after the turn of the century. The A.C. Dietsche Company issued a set of postcards featuring members of the Detroit Tigers in 1907. A similar edition was released the following year on the Chicago Cubs. Dietsche printed a set of Tiger photos in 1908 for the Detroit **Free Press.** A postcard set commemorating the 1919 champion Cincinnati Redlegs was issued in 1919 and 1920. Most of the sports subjects pictured in this early period, though, were various stadiums and playing fields. Two of the first were photos of the new Forbes Field in Pittsburgh, and the recently built Syracuse Stadium; both issued in 1909. The postcard, however, is more of a post World War II phenomenon.

Clubs began to issue postcards in the late 40's. The Cleveland Indians first release came in 1948. The St. Louis Cardinals printed one of the popular postcard sets first in 1950. Private photographers and printing companies have also become involved in the production of postcards. Photographer J.D. McCarthy has printed over 1,900 different postcards for players since the late 1940's. He has also produced cards for jockeys, football players, hockey performers and basketball players. Several other prominent photographers such as George Brace, Jim Elder, Mel Bailey and Doug McWilliams have been involved in the release of player cards. Companies such as Dormand, Dexter Press, Pan American and the Graphic Arts Service all have been involved in postcard printing at one time.

Cards included in this section are: those with postcard backs; postcard-sized pictures, not considered trading cards or premiums, issued by companies, clubs and individual photographers; and, exhibit cards from all years. This general classification may rankle the veteran collector, who for years has put these cards into two distinct categories, postcards and advertising cards; but it is being done with the hope that many will gain a more elementary understanding of this area of collectables.

As mentioned earlier, sports postcards came into great popularity in the years immediately following World War II. This was fueled by the fact that baseball was in a 'boom' period, and the players were becoming more fan oriented. Most major league teams, and many minor league, have issued postcards since the early 50's. They are given to the ballplayers to send to fans, or sold at the park. Most are now blank-backed, and seldom addressed and sent to persons requesting autographs as they were through the early 60's. They are now usually inserted into return envelopes. Sports postcard collecting is a natural out growth to the hobby of collecting autographs. So many of the postcards were returned signed that a collector soon had the beginnings of a postcard collection. To others, though, autographs detract from the actual value of the card.

Postcard values are derived from a number of factors. Scarcity is the primary variable. The Dormand card of Gil Hodges is presently in the collection of only a handful of hobbyists. Whether or not the card is autographed also dictates price. Autographed cards have a higher value to most postcard collectors. Age is not an important component, because older glossy cards usually turn off-color through age. Condition is important, but normally plays a lesser role in determining price. Postal cancellation machines damaged many cards sent through the mails, but many collectors have 'weeded' these out of their collections. Because there are few postcard checklists at this time, many of these cards will continue to be bypassed by some collectors. The many different croppings on some players' pictures, different poses, and multiplicity of issues all add to the problems in cataloging postcard issues. Until such lists are developed, postcard collecting will remain a secondary area within the sports collecting Hobby.

Sports exhibit cards first appeared in the early 20's, and were issued regularly until 1966. Many of the early exhibit cards contained postcard backs. Most were blank-backed, and the issues of 1962-63-64 included player statistics on the back sides. In addition to the baseball players pictured, Sports exhibits also featured boxers, wrestlers, and football players.

Exhibit cards acquired their name from the fact that many were printed by the Exhibit Supply Company, and, most were sold at county fairs and carnivals. The most popular subjects included movie stars and television personalities. Baseball personalities were also well-received by the public; evidenced by the fact that they were issued for 27 consecutive years. In the 60's, the appeared in dime stores in vending machines. Most of these anonymous issues were printed in Chicago and were run on cardboard sheets in multiples of 16. The majority of issues contained 64 cards, but with the exception of the cards issued in the last three years, it was difficult to definitely assign a date of issue to any card. The same pictures were often used, with slight differences in cropping, hat emblems and type used to print the players' names, for as many as fifteen consecutive years. Their eventual death was caused by threatened legal action against the publishers by some of the players pictured.

A sampling of different postcards is presented on the following pages. This area of the Hobby will most likely become much more sophisticated in the years to come.

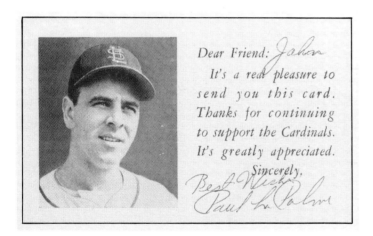

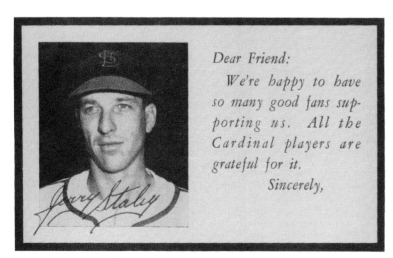

Postcards issued by the St. Louis Cardinals have a wide range of popularity. First issued in 1950, the Club has changed the format seven times. The first example, signed by Mr. LaPalme, was used in 1953-54-55. This is known as a 'Type Three' Cardinal postcard. The Haddix card, personally autographed across the photo area, was used in 1954-55. This has been classified as 'Type Four.' This Jerry Staley postcard, a 'Type Three,' also autographed, was issued in 1952.

Postcards picturing stadiums, arenas and other playing fields have been on souvenir racks since the early 1900's.

111

JOSEPH PAUL DI MAGGIO
NEW YORK A.L.1936 TO 1951

HIT SAFELY IN 56 CONSECUTIVE GAMES
FOR MAJOR LEAGUE RECORD 1941. HIT 2
HOME-RUNS IN ONE INNING 1936. HIT 3
HOME-RUNS IN ONE GAME (3 TIMES). HOLDS
NUMEROUS BATTING RECORDS. PLAYED IN
10 WORLD SERIES (51 GAMES) AND 11 ALL
STAR GAMES. MOST VALUABLE PLAYER
A.L.1939,1941,1947.

NATIONAL BASEBALL HALL OF FAME & MUSEUM
Cooperstown, New York

The Baseball Hall of Fame has issued postcards picturing the bronze plaques of inductees since the mid-40's. The first types were black and white. They are now brown on yellow background. There is a card for every member in the Hall. Very popular with autograph collectors.

One of the most popular player sets is the Dormand issue of 1954-55. It was one of the first releases that featured a full-color process. The card of Gil Hodges is as rare as any card that has ever been printed. The set featured mostly Yankees and Dodgers.

Cincinnati Reds

Picture cards printed by the various clubs are currently very common. These two examples show the diversity in design. The Reds included the players' facsimile signatures to make it even easier to answer fan mail.

This postcard was issued to commemorate Warren Spahn's 300th major league victory. It contains a facsimile autograph.

CANADA–U.S.S.R. 1974

This unique card was distributed throughout Canada. Fans were encouraged to write their best wishes on the reverse side and mail to the players involved in the Series with the Russians. The cards were pre-addressed, making it very easy for most to participate.

This Baltimore Oriole club-issued card is a part of one of the sets issued in 1960-63. Uniform styles can often be an aid in determining exact date of release.

James McCarthy of Birmingham, Michigan has been printing postcards for players in all sports since the late 40's. Close to 2,000 different baseball poses alone are known to exist. Note the "JMc" in the lower left corner of the Sandy Koufax card.

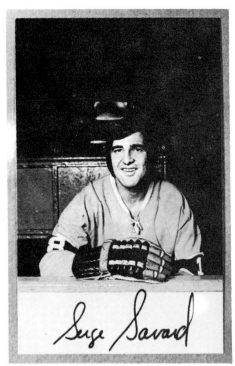

This set of club-issued photos were printed by the Montreal Canadiens. The signatures on the cards are facsimile.

This set of Hall of Fame exhibit cards is complete at 33 cards. Two different poses of Babe Ruth exist; explaining the discrepancy in the 'multiples of 16' rule.

Jim Rowe of Berwyn, Illinois produces postcards by using the thousands of original negatives he has acquired from various photographers. The player pictured is Johnny Mize.

Four examples of early exhibits are pictured in this sequence. Most exhibit cards contain the lines "Printed in U.S.A.," or "Made in U.S.A." Many of these early cards had postcard backs.

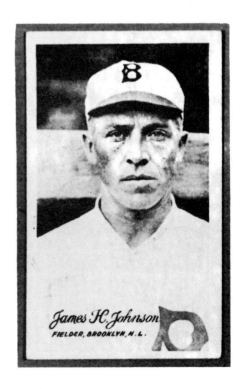

The player's uniform is often a tip-off as to the approximate year of issue. Norm Cash joined the Detroit Tigers in 1960.

The Cleveland Indians have issued postcards each year since 1948. For years, fans were able to receive a card of their favorite player by sending 10¢ to the Club. The real bargain was the fact that each came back personally autographed by the player pictured. These cards are now the source of many of the difficult, or deceased, players who performed for the Indians. A collector with a large supply of these cards probably has accumulated a greater fortune in autographs than he has in postcards.

There are 24 different members of the 1919 Cincinnati Reds' Championship team featured in this set. The card fronts are black and white. A similar version, with designation of "1919 National League Champions" across the bottom, was issued a year earlier; in 1919.

"HEINIE" GROH, *Captain and Third Base*
Cincinnati "Reds" World's Champions 1919

Exhibits with the line "Sincerely yours" appeared on the market for a period of three or four years in the late 40's.

116

Baseball personalities were not the only ones to grace the fronts of exhibit cards. Other popular subjects included boxers, football players, movie stars, television personalities and wrestlers.

Ty Cobb is one of six postcards that were issued by THE SPORTING NEWS in 1915. The set is very unusual for its time in that the photos feature pastel coloring. It is thought that these cards were available through a TSN offer.

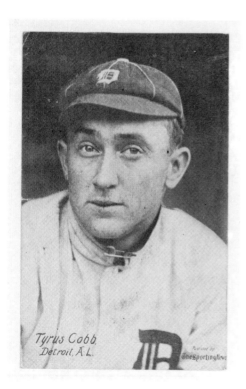

Individual hockey player postcards have long been sold at arenas. This sample was issued early in the career of superstar Bobby Hull. (Note Hull's uniform number.)

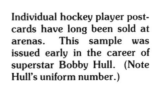

MELVIN THOMAS OTT

This sample is from a set of exhibits issued in the early 50's that pictured HOF members.

Photographer George Brace, of Chicago, has been shooting baseball player profiles for over 30 years. Many players have opted to have George's pictures made into postcards for their personal use. Pictured here is a shot of White Sox infielder Luis Alvarado.

Almost all recent exhibits contain the phrase Made, or Printed in the U.S.A. The 'printeds' are more prevelant. Baseball exhibits are also popular among autograph collectors.

118

Display Items

It is not uncommon to visit the home of another collector in which he has an entire room(s) full of sports memorabilia surpassed in size only by the Halls of Fame. Restaurants, taverns and game rooms across the country are also noted for these types of exhibits. In this chapter, some of the many such items that form those presentations will be pictured and described.

Many of these articles are one-of-a-kind items. Their uniqueness, as well as eye-appeal, make them popular additions to any collection of sports treasures. Uniforms and other equipment form a very important component of this larger, more encompassing area of display items.

These items are often found at antique shops and flea markets. Others were frequently used to promote, or decorate, sporting events. Some of them are quite valuable, others have a relatively inexpensive price tag. Value is determined almost exclusively by supply and demand.

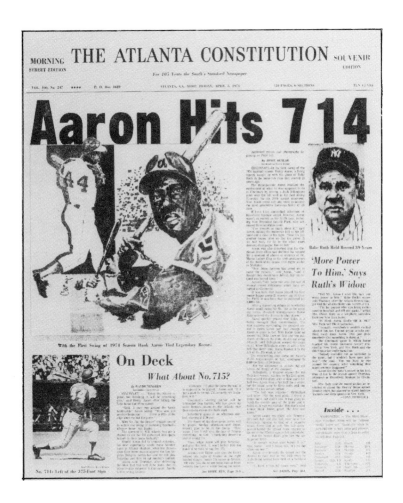

Colorful newspaper headlines such as this April 5, 1974 edition of the ATLANTA CONSTITUTION are found in many collectors' exhibits.

This reproduction of the front page of the September 27, 1940 DETROIT NEWS was used for a placemat by the Press Box restaurant in September of 1968 as the Tigers closed in on a long-awaited championship.

The full-page player profiles that appeared in the POLICE GAZETTE, when framed, or laminated as this one is, provide the best pictorial display of the performers of the early part of this century.

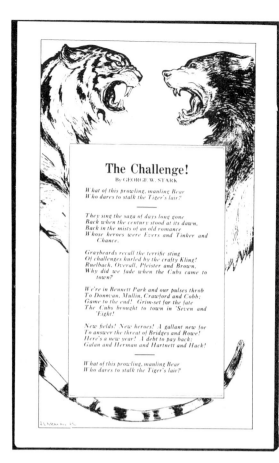

Original layouts from news- papers and magazines often find their way into the hands of collectors. This mat ap- peared, in smaller form, on the front page of the DETROIT FREE PRESS a few days before the opening of the 1945 World Series between the Tigers and the Cubs.

This bust of Baseball's Home Run King had a wide distribution. It first appeared during the 1974 season.

This plastic/rubber bust of Ty Cobb is one of twenty different HOF members in this set that first went on the market in 1963. The statues were produced by Sports Hall of Fame Incor- porated of Lynbrook, N.Y.

Old team photos, such as this 1902 pose of the Rollings College squad, make attractive displays.

Pictured in this sequence are four display bats. From bottom to top; a commemorative Hank Aaron bat that was given to purchasers of Magnavox televisions following the historic home run #715, two bats which were given to team members and club officials for the 1942 World Series and the 1940 All-Star Game, (similar bats have been presented to the teams each year by the Hillerich & Bradsby Company) and a special green bat that was sold to Oakland A's fans following their 1972 Series victory. The two Hillerich & Bradsby bats are shown in close-up form on the right.

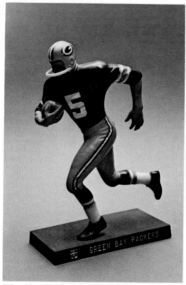

The Hartland Company also produced a set of football figures. The kit came with a panel of decal numerals so that the figure could be numbered as any player. The statue of the Los Angeles Rams and Baltimore Colts are actual palyers—Jon Arnett and Johnny Unitas.

A very popular item that is no longer being sold in its original form are these Bobbing Head dolls. Because of several toy safety laws, these plaster/composition figures were removed from the market. Pictured in this frame are dolls of varying values. The Mickey Mantle figure, along with several other players, appeared at concession stands in the early 60's. Dolls that feature specific players have a much higher value. The statue in the center, Seattle Pilots, has a slightly higher market price because the team has been dead since 1969. The Cincinnati Reds doll on the right is in a category with the other franchises that have been in continuous operation. The bobbing dolls have reappeared in recent years; made of a synthetic plastic.

One of the most popular non-card items is this set of plastic baseball statues that was produced by the Hartland Company. They were on the market in the late 50's and early 60's and usually sold for $1.98. Pictured in this frame are, from left to right, Stan Musial, Yogi Berra, Mickey Mantle and Hank Aaron. Some of the other notables in the series include Babe Ruth, Ted Williams and Willie Mays.

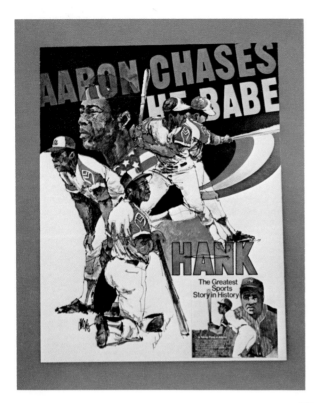

Posters that were issued on a limited basis, such as this Henry Aaron Poster Day item from 1973, have a wide collector appeal. Very few fans, less than 15,000, attended the game at which these were distributed. This particular copy has been autographed by Aaron, and includes a smaller drawing pasted in the lower right hand corner to cover the large logo of the sponsor.

Player's trophies, such as this 1967 Ty Cobb Award of Carl Yastrzemski's, often find their way into the collections of hobbyists. This trophy stands over three feet tall.

Lineup cards, such as this one from a 1974 California-Oakland game, that were taped on dugout walls, provide the collector with an authenic souvenir to add to his collection. The smaller blue lineup sheet is the type exchanged by the two managers prior to the start of the game.

This large 'W.F.' flag hung in the home of the Chicago Cubs—Wrigley Field. The Atlanta banner also waved atop the stadium roof. These are often available when new replacements have been bought by the club.

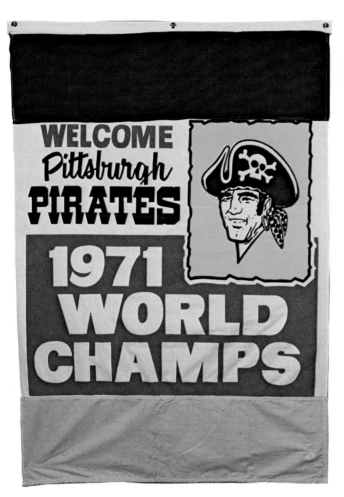

This square canvas banner was seen over the streets in downtown Milwaukee as a decoration for the 1975 All-Star Game.

This colorful banner hung in downtown Pittsburgh following the Pirates' 1971 Series victory. Pittsburgh has a long history of street decorating to commemorate their championship wins.

Fans attending the '74 All-Star Game in Pittsburgh also saw these banners that hung throughout the downtown and stadium areas.

The Pittsburgh Steelers' 1975 Super Bowl victory motivated the Chamber of Commerce to suspend these banners over several City streets.

The Atlanta Braves printed these distinctive certificates to give to those in attendance on the dates Aaron hit homers number 700, 714 and 715. Homer #714 was hit in Cincinnati, so the only distribution of this particular verification was to collectors.

Felt pennants have been a popular sporting souvenir since the turn of the century. These colorful banners often provide an added touch to a sports display. Pennants that are dated, those that mention specific events such as the All-Star Game, World Series, etc., have a higher value.

124

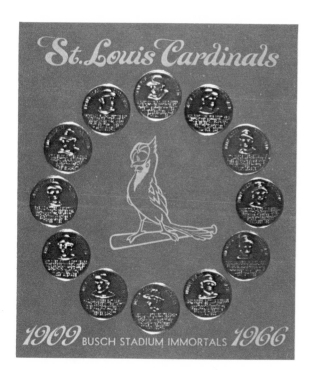

This set of twelve gold player coins, and display board, was distributed in 1966. Billed as "Busch Stadium Immortals," the edition includes great Cardinal performers.

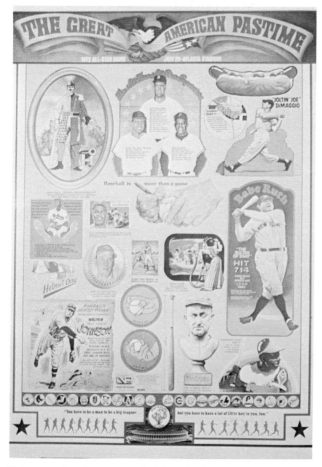

Colorful poster schedules from major universities and professional teams provide attractive additions to sports displays.

This promotional poster was distributed in limited quantities by the ATLANTA MAGAZINE to commemorate the 1972 All-Star Game.

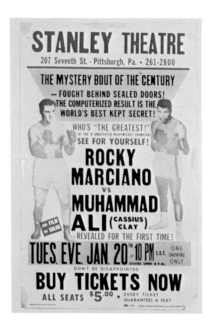

Boxing posters from great Ring match-ups have long been carried home from arenas by sports fans. Some of the older, larger boxing billboards are very much in demand.

Large movie posters from sports films become unique additions to exhibits of sports memorabilia.

This Al Kaline poster was given to fans who attended a game after the Detroit star had joined the 3,000 hit club.

126

Original artwork provides the collector with that 'one-of-a-kind' item that adds distinction to his accumulation of memorabilia. This work pictures Fran Tarkenton.

This small (10½") statue, dated 1910, is an original piece of sculpture. Items such as this are found in many collectors' exhibits.

Breweries often issue beer signs with a sports motiff. These two unique Indy 500 motiffs were issued in 1972 by Falstaff and Miller High Life.

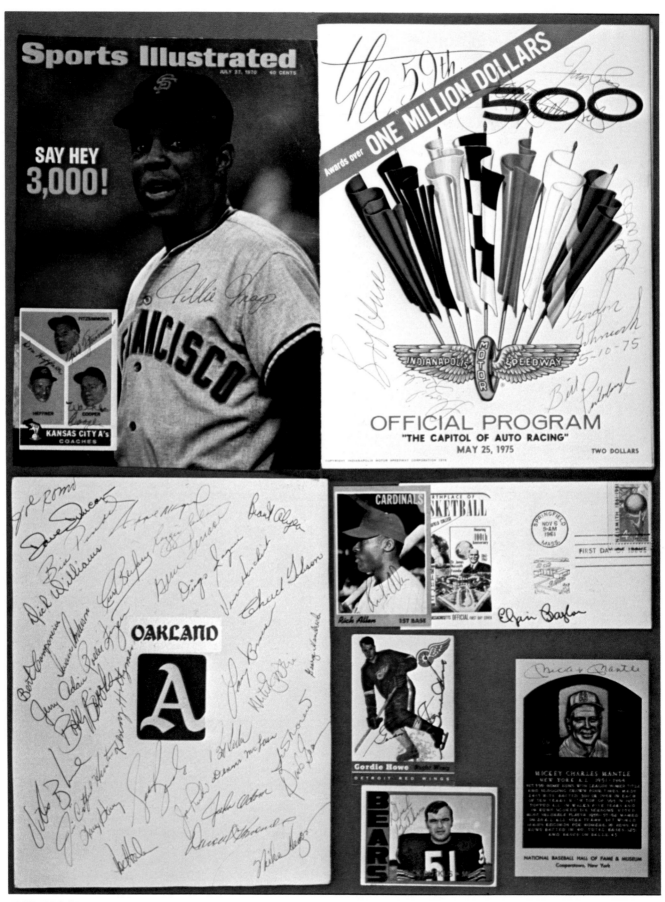

FOR DESCRIPTIONS, SEE PAGE 130

128

AUTOGRAPHS

One phase of the Hobby that has experienced a rapid growth of interest in recent years is autograph collecting. The reasons for this increased popularity are fourfold: first, this area of specialization is very flexible in that signatures can be obtained on a wide variety of material (index cards, photos, gum cards, programs, balls, etc.); secondly, autographs, as a general rule, are very easy to store or display; thirdly, autograph collecting, especially in baseball, is very organized. Address lists of past and present players are regularly sold, or printed in the hobby papers. Lastly, autograph collecting provides a certain challenge that is appealing to many collectors who wish to 'branch out' from card collecting.

The three most popular methods of collecting signatures are the 3x5 index card, the gum card, and glossy, or magazine pictures. Each has its own advantages and drawbacks. The index card signature's value is confined to the autograph itself. It is possible to use this method for any, and all players. They are easy to store and categorize. The gum card signature is presently the most popular. It is possible to significantly increase the value of your gum cards by having them signed on the front side by the player pictured. A relatively worthless set, such as the 1964 Topps Giants cards, signed by all 60 players would increase in value from $2 to approximately $75. The one drawback to card autographs is that not all players are pictured on the cardboard squares. While most players have been issued in recent years; this is not the case in sets issued prior to the mid 50's. Collecting signatures on photos is much costlier, not only for the picture, but for postage. As with the gum cards, not all players are easily located in picture form. The photos are also more difficult to store. As with any method used, a major disadvantage is the percentage of players who do not return the items you send them to sign. Losses can be calculated by adding the value of the items you have sent, plus the initial and return postage.

The values that are placed on autographs are much more arbitrary than those in other areas of sports collecting. Such variables as demand, availability, the date it was signed, the item the signature is affixed to, condition and authenticity are all used in establishing a market value. In many instances, the value can be determined by one of two denominators: is the player living or deceased? Because of this very 'cut and dry' categorization, autograph collecting has assumed the label of "morbid" in the estimation of many people.

Unlike values assigned to trading cards, a pattern of baseball supremacy does not exist in autograph collecting. Signatures of such athletes as Jim Thorpe, Jimmy Clark, Knute Rockne, Bill Russell, Jimmy Brown, Sonja Henie, Babe Zaharias or Paavo Nurmi would rank as equals in value, popularity and scarcity with their counterparts in baseball.

Autograph values fluctuate drastically depending, again, on the variables. An example of recent note is the case of Minnie Minoso, a former American League outfielder. Following his major league career, Minnie went to Mexico to play and coach. The value of a Minoso signature shot skyward to a high of $4-$5 in the summer of 1975. Collectors were unable to contact Minoso because of insufficient address data, and their inability to purchase Mexican stamps for return postage. In January, 1976, the Chicago White Sox announced that Minoso had been signed to coach their team. It is now possible to easily reach Mr. Minoso with autograph requests. There is no doubt that Minnie's signature will now drop near the 50¢ mark.

The above example may be applicable in the near future to the many former major league ballplayers who are living in Cuba. If diplomatic relations are re-established between the United States and Cuba, a large number of signatures that are presently demanding premium prices will fall significantly.

Besides the three major methods of collecting signatures described previously, there are a number of others that captivate the attention of collectors. Teamsheets, containing the autographs of an entire squad on 8"x11" or larger paper or cardboard, are becoming more popular. They incorporate the basic concepts of a team ball, but are easier to read, and store. Signed programs, or scorecards, have always been popular with collectors who obtain signatures in person after the game. Autographed balls, while losing appeal in recent years, are still an excellent source for team signatures of the first forty years of the 20th century. The ball itself is expensive, many do not hold up well through the years, and storage is a very real problem.

Autograph authenticity is a primary factor to value. If the signature is not authenic, it has no value. The vast majority of autographs are authenic. It is usually the very famous person that utilizes one of the three most common means of 'faking' an autograph. Because of the great volume of mail, or lack of time in their schedules, some athletes will use a rubber stamp, a machine that signs his name to documents, pictures, and other paper items (an autopen) or, will have another family member, secretary or friend do the signing. 'Stamped' signatures are usually very easy to detect. The other two illigitimate types are slightly more difficult to notice.

DESCRIPTIONS OF ITEMS ON PAGE 128 [clockwise]

- **Sports Illustrated** cover signed by Willie Mays. Signed covers from the **Sporting News** are also popular with collectors.

- 1975 Indy 500 program signed by drivers, including winner Bobby Unser.

- Basketball stamp first day cover signed by future member Elgin Baylor. FDC's are another fine item to secure autographs on.

- Gum card signed by Richie Allen. If you want a real challenge, try to get one of these!

- Signed gum card by hockey's "Mr. Everything," Gordie Howe. Howe has also excelled off the ice with fans for almost thirty years.

- Hall of Fame postcard signed by Mickey Mantle. Mr. Mantle's signature is one of the most sought-after. It is humanly impossible for him to answer all of his mail.

- Dick Butkus' signature on a football gum card. Butkus in no way resembles his antics on the field while signing.

- Teamsheet signed by the 1972 World Champion Oakland A's. Because this is a championship team, the value is higher than the common team signed sheet.

- Gum card signed by three coaches of the 1960 K.C. A's staff. Value increases as the number of persons signing increases.

Some collectors make the statement that, "Nothing, but nothing, is duller than a 3x5!" It is possible to 'doctor up' index card signatures by gluing small news or program pictures of the person to the card, as in this example of Bob 'Hunchy' Hoernschmeyer.

Many people feel that Johnny Longden was horse racing's greatest performer. He rode Count Fleet to the Triple Crown in 1943.

Signature of pro football Hall of Famer Steve Van Buren. Van Buren's autograph is somewhat difficult to obtain. Football HOF signatures are becoming increasingly popular with sports collectors.

In the last ten years many athletes have opted to change their names, for one reason or another. Probably the most famous to do this was the heavyweight champion of the world, Cassius Clay. A Clay signature would be worth 5-7 times that of an Ali; and will open up an even greater margin in years to come.

Collectors who have an autograph of Lew Alcindor now have a unique item. Alcindor has changed his name to Kareem Abdul-Jabbar; and no longer signs his name as he did during his college career.

An autographed baseball, signed by various members of the N.Y. Yankees. Values of signed balls are determined to a large degree on condition and age. A signature such as Mantle's will not hurt, either.

Pictured are three baseball HOF'ers on 'cut' paper. Christy Mathewson, deceased 1925, Frank Chance 1924, and Mordecai Brown, 1948, are all signatures that command premium values.

Christy Mathewson

Frank M Chance

Mordecai Brown

Rogers Hornsby

A 'cut' signature of baseball Hall of Famer Rogers Hornsby. Many signatures from this era were in pencil. Ballpoint pens were not yet in existence, although fountain pens were. Pen signatures are not as common, and increase the value of the autograph.

Piece of paper signed by baseball HOF'er Mel Ott, who was tragically killed in an auto accident in 1958.

Mel Ott

This reproduction featuring a Robert Riger drawing of Wilt Chamberlain is from an ad of The Equitable Life Assurance Society of the United States.

The 'New Breed' of athlete will often add a personal touch to his signature such as the 'Peace' on this Wilt Chamberlain autograph. The signature is on an Equitable sketch.

131

Supreme Court of the United States
Washington, D. C. 20543

One of the most difficult signatures to obtain in the world of sports is that of basketball center Bill Russell. Russell, who used to sign during his playing days, has changed his policy in recent years. This card, even in its trimmed, and surface-torn condition, would be highly prized by most collectors.

Occasionally, an athlete of renoun goes on to excell in another area of service. This signature of former Colorado All-America football player Byron 'Wizzer' White is enhanced as he is now a Justice of the Supreme Court.

There probably has not been a more well-known skier than Jean Claude Killy. His signature consists solely of his last name. This autograph is on an index card.

Signed gum card by the late Charles Dillion 'Cassey' Stengel. Many of Casey's later signatures were smeared, mispelled, or traced over. In the case of Stengel autographs, clarity is important.

As it is the case with cards, the most popular autograph among sports collectors is that of Babe Ruth. Ruth signed thousands of autographs during his life, but most people have opted not to part with them.

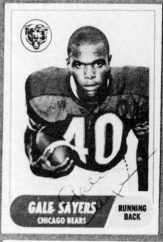

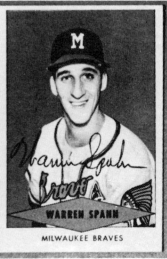

Signatures on gum cards is the current 'craze' of autograph collectors. The item you are obtaining the signature on, in this case the card, has an established value. The signature's value increases the total value of the card. With the new smear-proof pens that are now on the market it is possible to get nice, bold signatures such as those on the Eddie Leon, Bill Dineen and Ed Yost cards. Gale Sayers is already considered a football legend. The Stan Musial card is a relatively valuable card; the signature doubles its value. It is important that you are able to clearly read the signature. The Bob Turley card offers the signer a large, clear area to place his signature. Certain years of cards do not lend themselves well to autographs. Some cards contain facsimile autographs, which makes it even more difficult for the signer. (See 1967, 1971, 1955 Topps cards in card section for examples.) Willie McCovey is a difficult signature to obtain. This autograph, on a 1974 variation card, has considerably even more value. George Blanda's signature is in demand, but he helps the supply by obliging most all. Collectors interested in football HOF signatures have a difficult time getting Bobby Layne. The Warren Spahn card, a 1954 Red Heart, makes for a very attractive autograph.

Signed drawing of one of football's greatest performers, Johnny Unitas. This series of sketches, produced by the Equitable Insurance Company, provides collectors with a 'class' item to use for autograph collecting.

This Lee Trevino signature is on a small bumper sticker. Trevino, like many golfers, signs most requests.

No sports autograph collection would be complete without the signature of Baseball's Home Run King, Henry Aaron. Mr. Aaron obliged fans' requests for years. In 1973, when it became apparent that he would surpass Ruth's totals the influx of mail multiplied to the point where there were rooms full of unanswered mail. It would be safe to say that since 1973 there have been as many fake Aaron signatures as legitimate ones to enter the market.

Honk Aaron

Signed cut signature (from return envelope) of former Colt and Lion head coach Don McCafferty.

The Baseball Hall of Fame at Cooperstown, N.Y. has issued postcard-size pictures of the members' plaques for over 30 years. The first issues were black and white. They are now yellow bordered, with a mahogany-colored plaque. Hundreds of collectors have spent years obtaining the signatures of the Hall on these cards. This Sam Crawford card is on the black and white type; and, of course, has a higher value than the new colored variety.

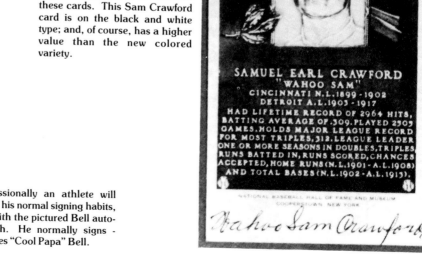

Ocassionally an athlete will alter his normal signing habits, as with the pictured Bell autograph. He normally signs - James "Cool Papa" Bell.

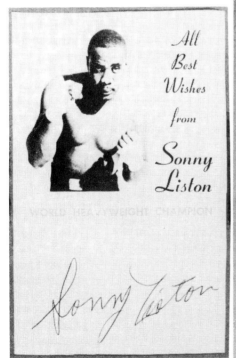

The heavyweight champion's autograph is in high demand by many collectors. It is said that Sonny Liston did not know how to sign his name until a year before his death. A legitimate Liston signature is rare in any form. Max Schmeling, the German champ, is cooperative, but difficult to locate. Muhammad Ali is common in this form. The legendary Jack ("Great White Hope") Johnson is a rare boxing signature. The tragic death of Rocky Marciano escalated the value, as well as the demand. James Jeffries was the champion from 1899 to 1905. Signatures from this era are difficult to find.

One of the most unusual signatures in the world of sports, or anywhere else, is that of NASCAR champion driver Richard Petty. Those who have received Richard's signature in person will attest that it takes quite some time for him to 'circle out' each masterpiece.

The demand for the signature of former UCLA coach John Wooden is high. Wooden willingly signs most all requests, keeping the supply fresh.

Detroit Tigers
1940

Del Baker   Bruce Campbell
Merv Shea   Earl Averill
Bing Miller   Pete Fox
Ralph "Red" Kress   Tom Seats
Barney McCosky   Ted Hutchinson
John Gorsica   "Dizzy" Trout
Dutch Meyer   "Hank" Steinbeck
Pinky Higgins   "Rudy" York
Schoolboy Rowe   Cliff Smith
Billy Sullivan   Archie McKain
Hal Newhouser   Tom Bridges
Hank Greenberg   Al Benton
"Birdie" Tebbetts   Dick Bartell
Frank Croucher
Chas. Gehringer

This is a signed teamsheet from the 1940 Detroit Tigers. This is a rare item, in this form, as the teamsheets have just recently gained acceptance. Many members of this team are now deceased.

ROBERTO CLEMENTE

Most Roberto Clemente signatures are not nearly as clear and precise as this one. His signature is normally very hard to read. His tragic death in a plane crash has escalated the demand for his autograph significantly.

136

A Minnie Minoso signature on a postcard-size photo. This $4 signature is now $1 in this form because of the circumstances explained earlier. No doubt, someday, it will again regain its value of a few years ago.

As with most boxers, the demand is high, the price is high; and the supply is low. James (Jas.) Corbett is no exception. In this postcard form, the collector has acquired a premium item. The fact that the signature is dated would also increase its value.

JAMES J. CORBETT.

An added chore for the autograph collector is to obtain more than one signature on a single item. As a general rule, signatures in this form increase to 1½ their value on a single signed piece. In this case, there would be little difficulty in obtaining three of the greatest hockey players around.

Some collectors find it an enjoyable pastime to get players to sign pictures that are not of themselves. This card of Frank Bolling is shown signed by Frank, left, and by his brother Milt on the right. The back of the second card contains biographical info on Milt. (See card descriptions, 1955 Bowman, for further details.)

137

David Forbes

For no other reason, at least at this time, the signature of Dave Forbes will be a collectors item. He was the first professional athlete to go on trial for an offense during a game; the court proceedings ended in a 'no decision.'

Connie Mack

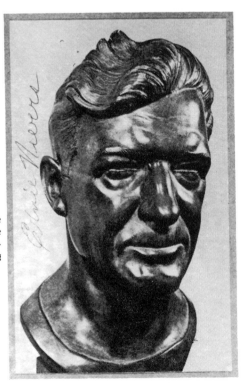

Lou Gehrig

Another signature that is almost equal in demand, but quite a bit lower in supply, is that of Lou Gehrig; Ruth's legendary teammate with the Yanks.

Connie Mack served Baseball for over 50 years; most in the capacity of manager and general manager. This signature is enhanced by the fact that it pictures Mr. Mack in his playing days. Mr. Mack's real name was Cornelius McGillicuddy. Signatures signed with the legal name have a greater value.

Often times the only way to obtain a signature of a person who has passed away is to secure a cancelled check from his family, or the club that employed him. This check, endorsed by Yankee owner Jacob Ruppert, and countersigned by now HOF'er Ed Barrow, was issued to pay for coal at Yankee Stadium in 1925.

Mark Spitz won seven gold medals at the 1972 summer Olympics. As with many other athletes, finding him is two-thirds of the battle. His signature will most assuredly increase in value as the decades roll on.

Mark Spitz USA

A pro football Hall of Fame bust postcard signed by Ernie Nevers. Nevers always cooperated with collectors seeking his signature.

138

(2) Upon receipt of the waiver request, any other Major League club may claim assignment of this contract at a waiver price of $1.00, the priority of claims to be determined in accordance with the Major League Rules.

(3) If this contract is so claimed, the Club shall, promptly and before any assignment, notify the Player that it had requested waivers for the purpose of terminating this contract and that the contract had been claimed.

(4) Within 5 days after receipt of notice of such claim, the Player shall be entitled, by written notice to the Club, to terminate this contract on the date of his notice of termination. If the Player fails so to notify the Club, this contract shall be assigned to the claiming club.

(5) If the contract is not claimed, the Club shall promptly deliver written notice of termination to the Player at the expiration of the waiver period.

(g) Upon any termination of this contract by the Player, all obligations of both parties hereunder shall cease on the date of termination, except the obligation of the Club to pay the Player's compensation to said date.

Regulations 8. The Player accepts as part of this contract the Regulations printed on the fourth page hereof.

Rules 9. (a) The Club and the Player agree to accept, abide by and comply with all provisions of the Major and Major-Minor League Rules which concern player conduct and player-club relationships and with all decisions of the Commissioner and the President of the Club's League, pursuant thereto.

Disputes (b) In case of dispute between the Player and the Club, the same shall be referred to the Commissioner as an arbitrator, and his decision shall be accepted by all parties as final; and the Club and the Player agree that any such dispute, or any claim or complaint by either party against the other, shall be presented to the Commissioner within one year from the date it arose.

Publication (c) The Club, the League President and the Commissioner, or any of them, may make public the findings, decision and record of any inquiry, investigation or hearing held or conducted, including in such record all evidence or information, given, received or obtained in connection therewith.

Renewal 10. (a) On or before January 15 (or if a Sunday, then the next preceding business day) of the year next following the last playing season covered by this contract, the Club may tender to the Player a contract for the term of that year by mailing the same to the Player at his address following his signature hereto, or if none be given, then at his last address of record with the Club. If prior to the March 1 next succeeding said January 15, the Player and the Club have not agreed upon the terms of such contract, then on or before 10 days after said March 1, the Club shall have the right by written notice to the Player at said address to renew this contract for the period of one year on the same terms, except that the amount payable to the Player shall be such as the Club shall fix in said notice; provided, however, that said amount, if fixed by a Major League Club, shall be an amount payable at a rate not less than 75% of the rate stipulated for the preceding year.

(b) The Club's right to renew this contract, as provided in subparagraph (a) of this paragraph 10, and the promise of the Player not to play otherwise than with the Club have been taken into consideration in determining the amount payable under paragraph 2 hereof.

11. This contract is subject to federal or state legislation, regulations, executive or other official orders or other governmental action, now or hereafter in effect respecting military, naval, air or other governmental service, which may directly or indirectly affect the Player, Club or the League and subject also to the right of the Commissioner to suspend the operation of this contract during any national emergency.

Commissioner 12. The term "Commissioner" wherever used in this contract shall be deemed to mean the Commissioner designated under the Major League Agreement, or in the case of a vacancy in the office of Commissioner, the Executive Council or such other body or person or persons as shall be designated in the Major League Agreement to exercise the powers and duties of the Commissioner during such vacancy.

Supplemental Agreements The Club and the Player covenant that this contract fully sets forth all understandings and agreements between them, and agree that no other understandings or agreements, whether heretofore or hereafter made, shall be valid, recognizable, or of any effect whatsoever, unless expressly set forth in a new or supplemental contract executed by the Player and the Club (acting by its president, or such other officer as shall have been thereunto duly authorized by the president or Board of Directors, as evidenced by a certificate filed of record with the League President and Commissioner) and complying with the Major and Major-Minor League Rules.

Special Covenants

Approval This contract or any supplement hereto shall not be valid or effective unless and until approved by the League President.

Signed in duplicate this _Seventeenth_ day of _January_, A. D. 195_6_.

_____ (Player)   KANSAS CITY ATHLETICS, INC. (Club)

118 Manor Street
Plainview, New York
(Home address of Player)   By _____ (Authorized Signature)

Social Security No. 101-24-4147   ——— Personnel Director ———

Approved MAR 12 1956 195_

William Harridge
President, American League of Professional Baseball Clubs

Many people rate him the greatest athlete of the first 50 years of the 20th Century. His life was as much legend as it was fact. His signatures today are in high demand, and low supply. To own a Jim Thorpe is the dream of many collectors. This tattered piece of paper, even in its obvious poor condition, would command a high price.

Besides the cancelled check, another way to obtain signatures of deceased persons would be to obtain old player contracts. This contract, in addition to the signature of Arnold Portacarero, contains the then American League President, and now HOF member, William Harridge.

Signature of the legendary Notre Dame football coach Frank Leahy.

Autographed footballs are usually a poor investment. The value of the football normally out weighs that of the signatures.

Few persons doubt that someday Rod Carew will take his place aside the other baseball greats at Cooperstown. Rod has usually been very cooperative with fans requesting his autograph.

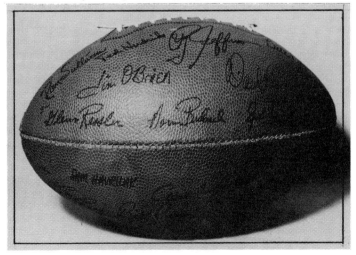

BOBBY HULL

For display purposes, and clarity, no method is better than the picture. The signer's autograph is normally larger in size, and is usually placed in an area that makes it easier to read. Two of the toughest Hall of Famers, Ted Williams and Jimmy Brown, and one of hockey's greats both on and off the ice, Bobby Hull, along with slugger Reggie Jackson comprise this sampling.

Other Items

In this chapter, various sports collectables of minor interest will be pictured and described. These items usually represent a secondary area of concentration to the collectors of cards, autographs or postcards. The vast majority of these items have been added to collections over a period of years. A few exceptions are the matchbook covers and pins, which in recent years have been checklisted to some degree.

The examples shown here are but a sampling of the countless sports-related articles that are considered 'collectables' by hobbyists. Countless other items could be classified in this section, but space restrictions will not allow their inclusion. This 'catch-all' chapter should give you a better understanding of the diversity that exists in the Hobby.

New additions to this set are being found each year. The pins were distributed by Orbit Gum in conjunction with their Tatoo Baseball Series. A second, unnumbered set was released the following year, in 1934. The unnumbered variety is in fewer supply.

Pins depicting defunct franchises have a higher collector interest and value.

Button pins issued at special events, such as player nights, have a greater value than other non-dated pins. The pins shown were issued on special days honoring Stan Mikita and Henry Aaron.

This commemorative pin was sold by the Pirates following the death of Roberto Clemente.

The manufacturer of these pins wanted to please everyone. These were popular in the City of Chicago during Leo Durocher's tenure as the Cubs' manager.

This Jackie Robinson pin was issued by the Topps Company with their 1956 baseball cards.

This pin was issued by the **New York News** to signal the return of Willie Mays to the City after his sale to the Mets.

Pins that include dates have a higher value than other novelty pins that do not. This 1958 Milwaukee Braves, and 1971 Super Fight pins are but two examples.

One of the most popular pin sets is the one distributed by Sweet Caporal cigarettes. They were issued in 1911 with other Company promotions, such as the trading card inserts.

This pin, issued in 1922, was distributed with Mother's Bread, a product of the Kolb Baking Company.

Superstar players such as Ted Williams were popular with the manufacturers of pin-backed buttons.

This pin of Al Kaline is one of 20 issued with Kelly's Potato Chips in 1969.

This pin featuring the now Muhammad Ali is part of a set of fourteen boxers.

142

Decals have long been a concession stand item at ballparks. The reverse side of this White Sox decal contains the 1941 Chicago schedule and was given away by the Club. The Cardinal decal, dated 1967, has a higher value than similar transfers because of this notation.

Adhesive stickers have replaced decals as the major type of transfer emblems. Shown here are four examples of team-produced promotional items. These often end up on children's bikes, notebooks, bulletin boards and car bumpers.

The franchise only lasted one year, and Pilots memorabilia is now very much in demand. This bumper sticker is an example of a concessions item that now has appeal with collectors.

Occasionally, stickers are dated. This 1972 Atlanta Brave sticker was used to promote the All-Star Game hosted by the Braves that year.

These pins were given to hydroplane fans at the various stops on the circuit by the boat's sponsor—Atlas Van Lines.

This Lou Gehrig pin is part of a 25-player set that was issued by an anonymous manufacturer in the early 1930's. Fourteen other HOF members are included in this group of drawings.

Can collecting is a current hobby rage. These two cans are examples of some of the sports subjects that have been issued. The can on the left was issued by Graf's Company to commemorate the 1975 All-Star Game held in Milwaukee. The Iron City Brewery has released several different beer cans that depict great moments in the history of the Pittsburgh Steelers and Pirates.

This large sticker was issued by the New York Yankees in 1973 to commemorate the 50th year of Yankee Stadium.

This metal 'license plate' is now a collectors item with the demise of the Fighting Saints' WHA team.

Matchbook covers often pictured sports personalities during the 1930's and 40's. Many years of work by veteran collector Frank Nagy has resulted in some twenty sets of these colorful items being checklisted. Hockey, football and movie star personalities appear in addition to the Diamond Heroes.

Pocket schedules are very popular with younger collectors. They are relatively inexpensive, and tradable with collectors in other parts of the country.

Older pocket schedules are now more difficult to find. Pocket schedule collecting is an area that has only recently found collector interest.

Various table games are also popular with some collectors. Games produced in the early 1920's through the 40's now bring good sale prices. Two of the most popular baseball table games are Strato-matic and APBA.

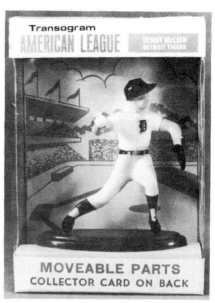

The cards on the backs of these Transogram boxes are much more collectable than the little figure themselves.

Postage stamps of many foreign countries picture sports personalities. Many of these countries issue the stamps to increase government revenues through sales to stamp collectors in other parts of the world. This set of three stamps was released by Fujeira to commemorate the first Ali-Frazier Fight.

Sports calendars such as this 1970 Marlboro edition also serve a functional purpose.

This key ring was sold at novelty counters in Kansas City and Omaha at Kings games.

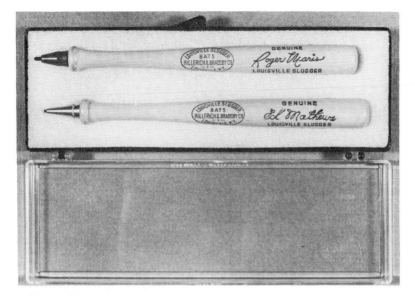

Minature Hillerich & Bradsby bat pens have been sold for many years. Popular players have a higher collector value.

There were 29 players pictured on this button set entitled "Our National Game." These buttons have a tab that should be bent back behind the picture in order to attach to clothing.

A 1974 Magnavox Hank Aaron 715 Club packet includes this pin of Baseball's Home Run King.

Newspaper accounts of memorable sporting events are saved by many collectors. Some collectors have albums of clippings on specific players or teams.

There are ten player pins in this set which was issued by the Hawthorn-Mellody Dairy. All players included are members of the Chicago White Sox. An eleventh pin denotes membership in the Club of Champions. They were issued in 1952.

Stereo records that recapture great sporting events have been released since the early 1960's. Most have been released by the Fleetwood Company of Revere, Mass. Most usually contain replays of actual broadcasts. Fleetwood maintains most selections in their present stock, so value is usually less than their present retail prices.

These replacement records are used with Mattel's Instant Replay football game.

This set of photo/records was first released in 1962. Each record includes interviews with the player pictured.

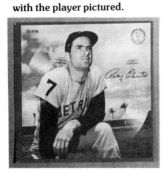

Those contributing to the fund to reno-vate the birthplace of Babe Ruth were sent this attractive gold coin.

These plastic coins, with paper center sections, were distributed in Canada with Salada Tea and Shirriff desserts. There are 120 coins in the set.

This set of 153 numbered coins was released by Topps with their baseball card set in 1971.

In 1963, Salada and Junket inserted these metal coins in their product boxes. There are 154 numbered coins in the complete set.

The Topps Company used these coins as inserts in their 1964 baseball card packages. There were 120 regular players, left, and 44 special All-Star coins, right. The coins are numbered.

These coins, issued in 1963, were inserts in boxes of Salada Tea and Junket Brand desserts. There are 63 players in the set.

This 1965 set of 40 coins, very similar to the Topps set of 1964, was issued in packages of Old London Corn Chips. The player coins are not numbered.

This aluminum coin was found on the inside front covers of the 1974 New Orleans Saints programs. The coins were part of a Burger King Promotion. A different coin was issued for each home game.

This set of plastic coins is complete at 221. The center sections are paper, and were distributed with Salada and Junket products in 1962.

This large pin was sold at the 1974 All-Star Baseball Game in Pittsburgh.

The Hobby/The Collector

Anyone over the age of 16 who mentions that he is a collector of sports memorabilia usually receives a puzzling look from his company. The general public associates the collecting of baseball cards and autographs on scraps of paper with those normally in grade school. The truth of the matter is that few persons under the age of sixteen are true collectors, but rather owners of accumulations of material. The sports collecting participants are actually a 'mirror' of the American population. There are physicians, lawyers, college professors, factory line workers, policemen, construction workers, clerks, secretaries, barbers, students and salesmen, to name a few, involved in this hobby. Age is not a common factor, as kids from 10 to old-timers of 90 are into this pastime. Race is not a common denominator, either; nor is nationality. The sports collector is a person with a little bit of 'child' left in him: people who enjoy reverting to a childhood remembered. For many, they have now found themselves in an economic position which affords them an opportunity to go back and purchase the 'toys' they never could afford as a child. Perhaps they first go back to buy what their mothers threw out when they were in high school. Not much as been written as to **why** people collect, but rather the **how** of all this.

To many of the 'Fathers of the Hobby' this recent influx of new enthusiasts has been received with mixed emotions. These veteran collectors can remember the days when the older cards sold for less than a quarter, the word of another collector was as solid as any contract, and the acquiring of cards and other items was simply a hobby, and nothing more. Many things have changed in the past twenty years and, in particular, the last seven.

The most prominent force in the Hobby since the late 60's has been the publications devoted to sports collectables. Hobby publications have existed since 1939, but their true impact was not felt until this recent period. The hobby papers were responsible for recruiting large numbers of new participants to sports collecting through their advertisements in other publications such as **The Sporting News, Street & Smith's** and other sports-related media. The hobby papers, in turn, exposed these new readers to the world of sports collecting. This simplified plot has run its course hundreds of times since. The Hobby is now so involved that the papers' influence on attracting new collectors is not as significant, although their role as the primary information source and policy maker has taken on new dimensions in the last few years.

Another factor that has led to the unprecedented growth of the Hobby has been the convention. First held in the early 70's, they are now held in almost every major league city annually. Many other less populated areas are also sponsoring these events. They are normally staged in a major motel/hotel with tables set up in the ballroom. Admission is charged to the general public and they are encouraged to bring in sports collectables for sale to the hobbyists. Sports personalities are present at most of these affairs to sign autographs and talk with the public. Auctions of premium material are held in the evening for the benefit of all collectors in attendance. Recent conventions have included seminars on various aspects of specialization within the Hobby. This facet will most likely play a more conspicuous role in the future as collectors grasp for more knowledge about the items in their collections.

An outgrowth of the convention has been the sports collecting club. A group of collectors sponsoring a convention can build from their base by accumulating the names of other local people interested in meeting on a regular basis. Several area clubs have become organized to the point of meeting every other month. Attendance at a number of these gatherings exceeds the number attracted to some conventions. Periodic newsletters are mailed to members, discounts offered on club-sponsored services, and car pools to other conventions are but examples of the advantages of membership.

Issues of importance routinely affect collectors and the Hobby. Amplified through the papers, most collectors become aware of their significance. Many of these 'problems' emerged with the growth of the Hobby, and have been present ever since. Prices have doubled, tripled, quadrupled, and more, on most items. Values printed in **The American Card Catalog,** published last in 1960, are but a fraction of today's asking prices. As late as 1967, 1955 Topps baseball cards were selling for 4¢ each, a set of '52 Topps baseball went for $160, and a Dan Dee sold for $5. These cards, in poor condition, bring a much higher price today. To some, this inflation will mark the death of the Hobby. To others, it is just another indication that all economic phases are undergoing drastic change. Another important issue that has been discussed for almost twenty years is the need for a new, updated catalog of sports cards, variations, publications, etc. **The American Card Catalog** not only does not contain listings for all of the cards issued prior to 1960, but, naturally, contains nothing issued since. A third meaningful issue is that of reprints. Reprints have become an area in which several dealers have applied themselves in the last few years. They claim that because prices for original material has sky-rocketed, they are not only justified, but are performing a service by printing reproductions for the benefit of those that cannot afford the legitimate items. Some argue that this is a travesty and reduces the value of all originals. An additional indicative problem is the abundance of publicity that has been generated throughout the country in newspapers, magazines and on television. This notoriety has been the source of thousands of new items falling into the hands of collectors. On the other hand, much of this hobby publicity leads the reader to believe that most, rather than some, items are of great value: escalating the prices paid to laymen for sports collectables. This, in turn, is another factor in the step-up market values.

The item of primary importance, though, focuses on individuals. Experienced collectors remember well the years when the integrity of the vast majority of those involved was unquestionable. With the admission of thousands of new participants into the Hobby, much has been lost. An analogy can be made between the small country school that becomes a part of a consolidation plan in which nine other units funnel in to a new building. Not only are there many new faces confronting the individual, but many unknown quantities. The following are common occurences: persons not paying for the items they bid on, and won, in mail auctions; persons 'bouncing' checks for items purchased; collectors offering in trade items that they hope to receive in another unrelated trade; collectors giving verbal assurance to another collector that items in question will be sold/traded to him, only to be informed the seller has received a better offer, cancelling the previous pact; collectors misrepresenting the items they are selling/trading; and, dealers/collectors either never sending merchandise ordered, or taking months to get it in the mails. Whether or not any such unscrupulous practices will change lies, again, with individuals.

In the interest of the Hobby, the following suggestions are offered. Perhaps this advice will serve as a guideline for your future dealings with others.

- How good is your word? If you agree on a transaction, uphold your end of it.
- When bidding in an auction — bid only what you can pay for and then pay for it when you are informed that you have the winning offer.
- When writing another collector — if you want a reply, list, etc. — enclose a stamp.
- Upon receiving a letter from another collector, always answer it if he has furnished a stamp for your use.
- If you cannot ship items you have advertised within a reasonable time frame (two weeks), do not advertise them. Wait until such time as your schedule will permit you to meet this commitment.
- If you receive items you are not satisfied with, do not hesitate to return them to the person who sold them to you. An explaination of your complaints should accompany the items.
- If a person who has received items from you in trade/sale is not satisfied, willingly accept them for refund or credit.
- Do not offer for trade/sale items that you do not own, and have readily available for shipment.
- Do not put items up for auction if you are aware of their market value (within 10%). Instead, list them for sale at that price.
- When holding an auction, make sure the rules are clearly stated for all participating.
- Accurately describe the items you have for sale/auction/trade. If unsure, opt the lesser classification.
- Ship items to other collectors as soon as your time schedule permits. An added incentive is not to cash the buyer's check until after you've sent the material.
- Remember, it is the responsibility of the seller to pay for insurance on shipping. The transaction is not complete until the buyer has received the merchandise, and the seller is responsible to that time.
- Treat others as you would want them to treat you.

Obviously, there will be other matters of importance that will surface in the future. A national organization, now in the discussion stage, may become a reality. Most collectors are presently not convinced that such a group would, or could, accomplish much. The legal battles over the rights to print players' pictures will no doubt occur between card publishers for years to come. Collectors and collecting clubs printing their own cards, or sets, will arise as these become more visible in the years to come. The labelling of certain players as 'superstars,' and the added values being assigned them will continue as a point of discussion. Likewise, the arbitrary ranking of card conditions will become more complex as the number of new collectors entering the Hobby increases.

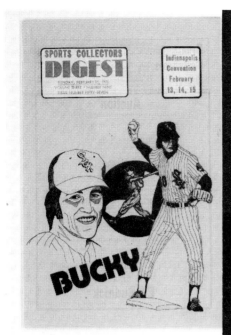

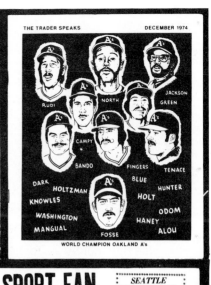

The Hobby papers, attributed with much of the recent growth in sports collecting, provide a 'soap box' for those involved. Similar papers have been published since 1939. Some of the papers in current publication are **The Trader Speaks**, which has the largest circulation; **The Sports Collectors Digest**, a magazine-type issue that appears twice monthly and contains news and ads; **The Sport Fan**, published since 1951, it is primarily filled with news and opinions; and **The Sports Collectors News**, which began printing in 1968 and includes news, views, and some advertising. Other papers are being introduced each year.

A sports collecting convention offers hobbyists the opportunity to buy, sell, and trade items with other enthusiasts. The public is also invited to attend.

153

Rich Egan

One of the most respected authorities in the sports collecting hobby is Richard S. Egan. His extensive efforts in indexing and checklisting most sports issues, primarily the older tobacco and early candy and gum releases, has formed the basis for much of the information that so many collectors now take for granted. It was not until the late 60's that accurate checklists of many card issues were developed.

Rich started to collect sports items seriously in 1955. As a child he can remember buying the first Leaf and Topps issues. It was approximately 1958 that he bought his first cards from a dealer; Sam Rosen, probably the hobby's first nation-wide card entrepreneur. "I bought what I needed to fill in my Leaf, Topps and Bowman sets. I can remember as late as 1961 buying Connie Mack All-Stars and current All-Stars for $5 each from dealers," Egan commented.

Once he had nearly completed the post WW II issues, Rich began to acquire some of the older cards. In 1961 he bought a collection that included hundreds of tobacco and caramel cards. Through Charles Bray's auction he acquired additional cards. "I wanted to get more of the caramel cards, so I wrote to other collectors. I found there were few checklists, so I began to compile my own. I really had very few of these cards at the time, but because of my correspondence, others began to associate me with cards of that type. When anyone I had contacted wanted to get rid of caramel issues, they would write offering them to me," Egan explained.

Rich has long been a writer for various hobby publications under his distinctive "Egan's Alley" title. He wrote regular articles for The Sports Trader from 1965 until it ceased publication; for the Sports Collectors News, The Trader Speaks and many others. "By 1973 most of the hobby papers had enough writers, so I decided to let someone else take over." His efforts shifted to the planning and implementing of the successful Chicago Baseball Nostalgia Expos. In June of 1975, the handful of previous convention organizers formed the Chicago-land Sports Collectors Association. That group now sponsors bi-monthly Saturday mini-conventions at which attendance by over 100 is normal. Egan acted as the group's first President.

Rich was graduated from the University of Illinois in 1963. In 1971, after eight years of additional study, he earned is PhD in chemistry. Since 1968 he has been employed by one of the country's largest pharmaceutical manufacturers as a senior chemist.

Now that he has completed many baseball sets that interest him, and because of the high cost of his needs, Rich has turned his efforts to items pertaining to the Chicago White Sox. "I collect anything on the Sox. I grew up in Chicago, and I've always been a White Sox fan. I've got hats, cards, yearbooks, press guides, and you name it.

Some of the old, large team pictures are unique such as the '06 and '17 Champions. My spring training press guides from 1927 and 1930, and the '34 and '35 yearbooks are also very uncommon. I'm now trying to get pictures of every Sox player, pictured in a Chicago uniform. I've got a good start, lacking only a few from 1940 to present. I'm putting them into albums by decades. It's something that has little investment potential, but I feel that the hobby should be for fun rather than profit. Most people wouldn't give me a dime for them, but they're what I want," Egan added.

Mr. Egan is married, and the father of three children. "My oldest child, Mike, is also a collector. He's helping with the albums. It's now a family project." Rich's two daughters may one day also join the hobby, but are presently too young.

An example of the 'true collector,' Egan summarizes his feelings toward the Hobby, "I've never been interested in the monetary aspect of this thing. On the other hand I'm not a stupe, and won't give things away. I wish though, that everything wasn't so expensive. The 'cut-throat' aspect, and 'everybody out for himself' attitudes are also ridiculous. To me it has to be fun. If it's not I'll find something else to do with my time."

Marty Craft

To many fellow collectors Marty Craft is just another name on the long list of sports enthusiasts. Few know that Marty's full name is Martha, and that she is one of the ever increasing number of females who have entered the hobby in recent years.

"I was afraid at first that I would get a negative reaction from the men collectors. I like being accepted as a collector. Most of them take you at face value so it makes little difference. I've used 'Marty' on all of my hobby correspondence since I started," Martha commented.

Marty was born in Michigan, and as a child collected clippings of the Detroit Tigers. It wasn't until 1970 that her brother Bob introduced her to the 'original' area of the hobby. "He would bring me the hobby papers and card catalogs, and my interest increased. We started to attend the Detroit convention together, and have been going ever since," she added.

Since 1971 she has been an executive secretary to a department director at a large Ann Arbor, Michigan hospital. In her spare time she has accumulated over 300 hardcover books on baseball, thousands of gum cards and old Tiger player photos. She has an excellent collection of photos of the 1935 Detroit team, and is presently working on a Hall of Fame album. "Each page is reserved for one member. I've found as many different photos, clippings and cards of the members as I could. It's been a bigger project than I anticipated, but it's going to be something very unique when it is complete," replied Marty.

"I got into too many different areas all at once. If I had to do it over again I would read the hobby papers for a few months and see what's happening. I have all kinds of gum cards from the 60's. I now might phase out the cards, but there really is nothing there that is valuable. If someone made me an offer I'd probably take it. I even have some football cards that were given to me by kids in the neighborhood. Patients bring me old clippings. It's hard to recognize what you want to collect without trying each one; but if you can, you'll save yourself a lot of money."

Like all collectors, friends are quick to 'needle.' "They all kid me at work about saving this stuff. It's not derogatory, but all in good nature," Martha explained.

Asked about women in the hobby, she commented, "I really haven't met any other female collectors. To a great degree many of the wives of collectors are just as involved in their husband's hobby as he is. They have the knowledge to go around at a convention and find the items that are valuable, or what their husband needs to complete a certain set. More women will enter the collecting thing in the future."

Marty's main interest is with the player of the 20's and 30's and 40's. "I like the old timers. "They're fascinating. The pictures, the clippings, the cards, all bring to mind some interesting story. It's all a lot of fun."

Dan Even

Dan Even, like most every young boy, bought baseball cards each summer. He remembers his first purchase in the summer of 1953. He laid them aside as other activities began to take preference in the late 50's. In 1961, he got involved in the 'organized' hobby of sports collecting.

He became interested in postcards, and club-issued pictures in 1962. He would spend hours writing to each of the players for an autographed return. Now, he not only has one of the better postcard collections in the hobby, but quite a few valuable baseball signatures.

There was a time, though, when Even's fascination with sports collectables was of secondary importance. "I kind of dropped out of things from 1970 until the Chicago convention of August, 1974. I was busy working, with things at home, and hadn't gotten rid of anything," Dan commented.

Dan was born in Dubuque, Iowa. He attended Loras College in Dubuque, graduating in 1965. He went to work for newspapers in Dubuque, and Clinton, Iowa before joining the Associated Press staff in 1970. He is married, and the father of four girls.

Another aspect of Dan's impressive collection are his baseball blankets. "I started to collect these, too, in the early 60's. I bought quite a few through mail auctions, and got others through trades. There are 187 known versions. I now have all but nine," Even explained.

Dan has spent considerable time over the years writing articles for the various hobby-related publications. "I think I wrote for all of them at one time or another. I finally stopped, mainly because of other time committments. I'd like to, but just don't have the time. I plan to turn in some of the checklists I've been compiling with other collectors on some of the major postcard issues," Even added.

Dan also has an extensive library of the old sports hobby papers. "I've subscribed to many since 1960, and thought it would prove interesting to go back and get all of the older issues. You can see how this hobby has evolved by looking at the publications. There is the **Card Collectors Bulletin,** published since 1939. The old issues contain most of the additions to the **Card Catalog.** There was **Card Comments,** which began publishing in 1958, **The Card Collector** which started about the same time, and **The Sport Hobbyist** whose first issue came out in 1950.

After the Second World War there was a Hobby-Fan paper, **The Trading Post,** which had a selection for sports collectables. Bob Jasperson's **Sport Fan** began in 1951, and I have all of those issues. The current papers are quite a bit more sophisticated than the publications from the hobby's infancy." Dan commented.

"There have been changes, Even noted," some good, and others bad. Most of the guys you used to deal with were interested in trading; now, most are concerned with sales. Collectors know more about the availability of items now, because of the large amount of advertising in the papers. I'm not saying, though, that the average collector knows any more about what he is collecting. Many collectors still have little knowledge of the items in their collection. There is probably as little research going on now, as in the past. The conventions are good. One of the biggest changes has been in the emergence of new fields. Collectors of autographs, yearbooks, uniforms and some of the other non-card items are a recent phenomenon. I think the reprints are a bad aspect; and there'll be more as the years go on, and prices go up. Too many guys are in it for the buck, but that's the reality of the situation. I'd say 90% of the guys you deal with are good. In the 'old days,' though, I never once was 'stung' on a deal. That isn't true anymore."

Even has also been very active in the formative years of The Great Plains Sports Collectors Association, a collecting group with members in an eleven-state region.

Glossary

advertising pieces — usually large cardboard stand-ups that were used in window displays. They included portrait, or action shot, of sports personalities and promotional copy for products or events.

auction — a sale of materials to the highest bidder. Most auctions of sports collectables are conducted through the mails. Live auctions are held at most sports conventions.

autopen — a machine that is used, primarilly by persons in government or entertainment, to sign documents and autograph requests. Autopen autographs have no value to a collector.

blankets — cloth fabric inserts, usually 5-8 inches in length, that contain pictures, designs, drawing, etc. of various subjects. They were distributed as inserts in the tobacco packages of the early Twentieth Century.

Bowmans — (BO-mans) cards issued by the Bowman Gum Company of Philadelphia, Pennsylvania from 1948-1955.

caramel cards — a common classification given to trading cards that were inserts in candy products in the 1900-1930 period.

card catalog — the **American Card Catalog,** last published in 1960. This reference work is a general listing of most paper items issued prior to 1960.

cereal cards — a term used to classify cards that were issued with breakfast food.

check — a cancelled bank note bearing the signature of a sports personality. Checks are often secured from the family of a deceased person for autograph purposes.

club-issued postcards — pictures of players, usually blank-backed, that are produced by the team they play for. Players often send these to fans requesting autographs.

collector-issued cards — sports trading cards and postcards that were produced and printed by a collector for the purpose of sale or distribution to other collectors.

condition — the existing state of any item. The most accepted spectrum includes: poor, fair, good, excellent and mint.

cut — a piece of paper, usually smaller than three inches by five inches, containing an autograph. Cuts are often seen which are slightly larger than the signature itself.

dealer — a person who sells sports collectables as a source of primary, or secondary, financial income. Most dealers are also collectors.

Diamond Stars — common term for baseball cards issued by the National Chicle Company from 1934 to 1936.

'E' cards — trading cards issued with gum and candy in the 1900-1930 period. 'E' is used as a prefix for these cards in **The American Card Catalog.**

errors — an item, usually cards, that contains a mistake: inaccurate statistics, incorrect pictures, wrong numbering, inaccurate ink colors, etc. If these mistakes are corrected by issuing another card(s) they both then become variations.

exhibit cards — postcard-size, usually blank-backed, cardboards that were seen frequently in vending machines at county fairs, carnivals and bazaars.

Fatimas — (Fa-TEE-mas) cards issued by the Liggett & Myers Tobacco Company with their brand of Turkish cigarettes in the early 1900's.

Goudeys — (Gow-dees) cards issued by the Goudey Gum Company of Boston, Mass. in the 1930's.

gum cards — trading cards that were issued with chewing gum products.

HOF — a standard abreviation for 'Hall of Fame.'

hot dog cards — trading cards, most always regional in nature, issued by meat companies with their weiner products.

Kahn's — (Conns) trading cards issued by the Kahn Meat Company with their hot dog products.

Leafs — trading cards issued by the Leaf Gum Company of Chicago in the late 1940's.

media guides — booklets printed by colleges, professional teams, and major sporting events for the primary use of reporters, announcers and commentators. They include individual statistics, team records, schedules and other pertinent information.

Old Judge — trading cards that were also stiffeners in packages of the Goodwin Tobacco Company's best-selling product: Old Judge cigarettes. The smokes were sold in small wooden boxes.

plaques — postcard pictures of the bronze plaques of each player in Baseball's Hall of Fame at Cooperstown, New York.

Play Balls — common term for trading cards issued by Gum, Inc. of Philadelphia, Pennsylvania in the 1930's and early 1940's.

premiums — items that were made available to the public by redeeming coupons, wrappers, boxes, cards, etc. These items were usually advertised on a trading card or product wrapper.

programs — booklets of more than four pages that were sold as a fan's 'guide' to a sporting event.

regionals — trading cards that were distributed only in a city, or small geographic area of the country. These sets usually pictured only players popular in the distribution area.

samples — a common term given to sports uniforms that were not the property of the club and/or were never worn by the athlete. They usually show little or no wear; often difficult to differentiate from authenic uniforms.

scorecards — a 'guide' to a sporting event that is less than five pages in size. Usually sold at baseball games, and four pages in length.

SI — a common abbreviation for **Sports Illustrated** magazine.

silks — fabric pieces that contained colorful designs, drawings and pictures of various subjects. These were inserted in packages of cigarettes in the early 1900's. Usually 4-6 inches in length.

stamp — a term used to describe a signature that was affixed by a molded rubber device. Stamped signatures have no value to an autograph collector.

stub — the portion of a ticket to a sporting event that is given back to you by the ticket taker. Stubs have less value than a full ticket.

superstars — an arbitrary category established by dealers which places a higher monetary value on the cards of popular players such as Mantle, Ruth, Gehrig, Mays, Aaron, etc.

'T' cards — trading cards issued with tobacco products. 'T' is used as a prefix for these cards in **The American Card Catalog.**

3 x 5 — term used to describe an index card that is three inches wide and five inches long. Popular with some autograph collectors.

ticket — the admission pass to an athletic contest. Full tickets have a greater appeal and value than stubs.

tobacco cards — term used to describe trading cards that were inserted into packages of tobacco products. Most were issued from 1878-1918.

Topps — cards issued by the Topps Chewing Gum Company of Brooklyn, N.Y. and Duryea, Pennsylvania from 1950 to present.

TSN — abbreviation for **The Sporting News,** a weekly, national sports publication.

T-205's — a common name for trading cards in the 1911 Gold-Bordered Baseball Series issued with tobacco. This code number was assigned to this series in **The American Card Catalog.**

T-206's — a common name for trading cards issued in the 1909-10 White-Bordered Baseball Series with various tobacco brands. This code number was assigned to this issue in **The American Card Catalog.**

TTS — a common abbreviation for **The Trader Speaks,** a monthly hobby publication edited by Dan Dischley of Lake Ronkonkoma, N.Y. It has the largest circulation of any of the sports collecting publications.

variation — a trading card of which at least two, and possibly more, different versions exist. At least one usually contains some type of error: printing, statistical, etc. Once an error card has been corrected by issuing a corrected version, both cards then become variations.

Index